Designed, Edited and Published by:

Celebrity Profiles Publishing

Richard and Madeline Grudens

Box 344 • Stony Brook • NY• 11790-0344

celebpro4@aol.com

www.RichardGrudens.com

Library of Congress Control Number in Progress

ISBN: 978-0-9847878-4-5
Printed in the United States of America
King Printing Company Inc., Lowell, MA 01852

Books and CD's written and/or produced by Richard and Madeline Grudens

The Best Damn Trumpet Player
The Song Stars
The Music Men
Jukebox Saturday Night
Snootie Little Cutie - The Connie Haines Story
Jerry Vale - A Singer's Life
The Spirit of Bob Hope
Magic Moments - The Sally Bennett Story
Bing Crosby - Crooner of the Century
Chattanooga Choo-Choo - The Life and Times of the World-
Famous Glenn Miller Orchestra
The Italian Crooners Bedside Companion
When Jolson was King
Star*Dust - The Bible of the Big Bands
Star*Dust CD
Mr. Rhythm - A Tribute to Frankie Laine
The Lee Hale Story
Sinatra Singing
Perfect Harmony
The St. James General Store
Radio Man - The Diary of Frankie Dee

RADIO MAN

Recollections of Frankie Dee

Keeper of Yesteryear's Musical Flame
Burning Brightly at GMMY World Wide Radio

RADIO MAN

Recollections of Frankie Dee

Table Of Contents
I Recall...

DON'T QUIT
Don't Quit No Matter What!

When things go wrong, as they sometimes will,
When the road you're trudging seems all uphill,
When funds are low and the debts are high,
And you want to smile but you have to sigh,
When care is pressing you down a bit,
Rest if you must, but don't you quit.

Life is queer with its twists and turns,
As every one of us sometimes learns,
And many a failure turns about,
When he might have won if he'd stuck it out.
Don't give up, though the pace seems slow -
You may succeed with another blow.

Often the goal is nearer than
It seems to a faint and faltering man;
Often the struggler has given up
When he might have captured the victor's cup,
And he learned too late, when the night slipped down,
How close he was to the golden crown.

Success is failure turned inside out -
The silver tint of the clouds of doubt,
And you never can tell how close you are -
It may be near when it seems afar;
So stick to the fight when you're hardest hit -
It's when things seem worst that you mustn't quit.

This poem was presented to me 30 years ago by my elder peers of spiritual sobriety.

About Frankie...
The Recollections of an Unusual Man

These are the recollections of an unusual man who loves his friends and loves his lifes efforts in so many areas. Frank DeSimone, known to one and all as Frankie Dee, or Frank E. Dee - has shown his reverence clearly through the following pages.

From his work in Boston with his mentor, Bill Marlowe, you are taken through what he calls "A New Beginning" after his battle with alcohol. His romance with his still standing GMMY Radio that entertains the world from his headquarters in California though satellites in Italy, England, and a handful of stations in America, where the music of the thirties through the Sixties dominates.

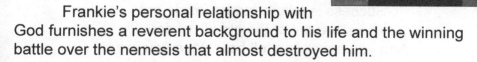

These recollections trace his "good old days" in the Boston Area where he grew up. His relationship with Bill Marlowe and broadcaster Ron Della Chiesa, as well as interviews with singers and personalities of the era that include Buddy Clark, Kitty Kallen, Jerry Vale, Al Martino and others - all are pleasant reads.

Frankie's personal relationship with God furnishes a reverent background to his life and the winning battle over the nemesis that almost destroyed him.

Here you will meet the friends of his life and rejoice with them in intimate detail. I trust you will enjoy his regular, thoughtful stories as much as I did.

Read on my friends.

Richard Grudens

Stony Brook, New York

The Statistical Page on Frank E. Dee

Gender: Male

Industry: Non Profit

Occupation: Radio Host

Location: Costa Mesa, California

Favorite Movies: Old Clean Movies of the past

Favorite Books: by Author Richard Grudens

Favorite Music: Big Bands and singers of The 1930's, 40's, 50's and 60's.

Blogs I Follow: GMMY Radio

About Me: GMMY Radio is a labor of love, a non-profit radio station, broadcasting around the globe, the nostalgic songs of the 30's, 40's & 50's. We keep those songs and big band music alive.   Visit www.com/Gmmyradio.htm.

I RECALL

The Good Old Days and Growing Up Italian

Remembering the Victory Gardens?

Growing a victory garden was the norm back then. My senior friends, whom I get together with often, talk about the days when our parents used to cook on a black stove in the kitchen with wood or coal, and there was no such thing as a refrigerator, nope! An ice box was where we kept food cold. It worked, but it required ice which was cheap.

Food Grown From an Italian Garden

Being raised by Italian parents - from Italy, you can be confident that whatever my mother cooked - it was all homemade.

Back then they made homemade Italian bread and homemade pasta, and for salad, they used to go dandelion and mushroom picking as well. The dandelions were either used for an Italian salad, or cooked like spinach with olive oil and garlic. If the dandelion was used for a fresh salad, then imported olive oil was used with homemade vinegar made from my father's homemade wine.

Everything that was going to be cooked and set on a table, where we dined in my parents' home, was homemade. We seldom bought at any store, as a matter of fact I never recalled seeing any cans of store-bought vegetables ever being brought into my parents home. Everything came from the garden and was put up in jars.

My parents, like other Italian families of the 40's and 50's, were certainly not spenders. Who had money to spend in those years? I can recall my parents growing peppers and then adding them into a big ten pound vat with homemade vinegar to marinate for a few weeks. Good grief! My father used to get angry at me whenever I ate one of those peppers, because I would make crazy comments like, 'pa, these peppers will grow hair on any one's head!" He certainly did not find my humor funny. However vinegar peppers were also used in salads and also used to fry with eggs for an Italian omelet.

My mother Emilia and my kid brother Leo

Growing A Garden Is A Labor Of Love

I'm often asked by friends "where do I find the time to grow a garden, isn't that too much work?" Well everything in life we do seems to be a full time job, however if one decides to grow a garden it is truly a labor of love. I grow a garden because I was brought up by my parents who grew a back yard garden and a farm garden. All of my family members were handed a spade to dig the soil and turn it over. Having a local yard garden was part of our family living especially if we wanted to eat fresh vegetables. In the 1940's and early 50's, there were no such thing as buying a automatic plow, and in no way did any of us in the family ever bring up buying a motor type plow. If this was brought up to my father, he was quickly vocal "get on the end of that shovel. Less talk and more digging." For sure we were told what to do and when to do it.

As I look back to those years I remember we lived on fresh vegetables that we grew from our Victory Garden, and the law from my father was to share our vegetables to those who did not have a garden. I still follow my father's law of giving and not taking. In this society I see a lot of takers and very few givers, and I see the materialistic people who complain and complain and certainly do not go out of their way to offer a cup of coffee. Those of us who remember the forties and early fifties, local neighbors in our neighborhood welcomed one another for coffee or a perhaps soda.

Recently, speaking to a group of wonderful seniors, they recall the Victory gardens or a vegetable garden in their back yard, and they shared with their friends who weren't able to grow a garden often due to having no land on which to grow vegetables.

As long as I'm on this earth and able to grow a garden, I will continue to do what my father taught all of us seven brothers and one sister to do - "share your garden with those who do not have a garden."

How Can People Sell a Garage and Yard Without the House?

During those beautiful New England summer years of the 1950's, I'll never forget the weekends. My father would always ask me to drive him to his personal garden situated on land, owned by my Uncle, who graciously allowed my father to work the land to grow his hearty vegetables. In those days, I owned a 1950 Buick, and from where we lived the ride to the farm was about twenty minutes. As we drove along the scenic back roads of Lexington to get to that large garden and those immense two-pound tomatoes, I recall that it was a lot of hard work to maintain an acre of land - we had to remove weeds and we would gather every imaginable vegetable for our home and we even shared with neighbors. My mother worked so hard to put up tomato sauce into jars for the coming winter months.

Every time my dad had the urge to go to the farm to pick vegetables or remove weeds, he would ask me to get the car ready to go. He always made sure to bring along a few gardening tools to help remove weeds. I would crank up the car and my father would slip into the front seat, and once he shut the front door, he was quick to ask me to get the car going. I would start the engine and race the motor on purpose without actually driving off. The car would shake and my father would look at the sidewalk and then glance at me wondering why the car was not moving. He would become angry and yell out "are we going today or another day." When it came to humor my dad never cracked a smile.

I always would take short cuts to go to the farm and usually return a different way to our home. My father could not speak English well, and to read signs such as 'house to let' or signs that read 'garage sale' or 'yard sale' it would completely baffle him to no end. As I drove along he would ask me to pull over because he saw a sign that read 'yard sale.' His comment, in broken English, to me was: 'how's can thesa peoples sella theira yard or garages without the house? How stupid are these people'? I always found myself getting angry at my father in trying to explain that the yard was not for sale nor was the garage. But I always lost out. Because he believed what he had seen with his eyes what he read. When we would arrive home, my father was quick to report to my mother that he saw signs that people were selling 'House To Let' which he thought was a toilet being sold. I had to explain to my mother in Italian what it meant. She always understood even though she too could not speak English too well, therefore to avoid anger traveling back and forth to the old farm, I took various roads that had no real estate or houses or any signs that read 'for sale.'

We never saw a Du Mont Television

Growing up in the 1940's and 50's, television sets were unknown to those of us before we reached our teens. We had not heard of what a television was until we first saw one at the local fire station in our area. We used to call the fire station The Fire Barns. That same fire station still exists in our old neighborhood. This fire station became an entertainment station for us young boys who never saw a television show on a television set. The size of the screen was about 10 inches wide and 10 inches in height with an attached magnifying glass to make the screen look about 14 inches wide. Some of the magnifying lenses were attached to the face of the set, and some came in various colors like red, blue, green and yellow to give the viewers the effect of color as if they were watching a color movie at a theater.

The firemen were so kind in allowing us young boys to watch television. Before we were allowed to view television, the firemen would always asked if we were good boys and they let it be known that bad boys were not invited to view their television. We, as young boys were amazed to see what television was, and we were-fascinated because we never saw a television and no one in our neighborhood had a television in their home, because it was the so called new 'in thing,' and mostly no one could afford a television.

Our first TV show was 'Howdy Doody' and of course cartoons. The gracious firemen regularly invited the neighborhood boys to watch television for a few hours. The firemen even reserved a few rows of seats for us. We had never heard of Du Mont TV Studio, that featured a lot of shows for kids as did NBC.

As we grew older we became good friends with the firemen,

and often in later years we would visit them, and those who retired we will never forgot their kindness to a bunch of young boys who viewed their first television show.

Here Comes The Milkman, The Ice Man
The Vegetable Man, And The Bread Man
The Great 1940's and 50's Home Deliveries

For those of us who grew up in the 1940's and 50's you will no doubt remember when the milkman and the ice man made home deliveries. The iceman delivered a block of ice twice weekly for our ice box. God help those of us who had to empty the large pan under the ice box filled with melted water from the ice. Guess who use to empty the water pan under the icebox? I remember my father telling me "don't spill any of that water on the kitchen floor that has just been waxed!" If you were to ask any young teen now about this era of time, they probably wouldn't know what an ice box did? My old ice box is being used to hold household tools in my brother's basement!

In those early years you would see horse drawn wagons filled with all types of vegetable and fruits - and in those days fruits and vegetables were sold by the dozen and not by the pound. The vegetable man use to sing out "get your fresh oranges and apples .20 cents a dozen." I recal seeing every woman in the neighborhood come out of their house and walk over to the horse drawn wagon to pat the horse and while patting the horse they would get to eat free fresh fruit before they bought anything.

I worked for the milkman, Bill Martines and his brother Frank, who owned the dairy called 'Blue Ribbon Dairy Farms' helping deliver milk to homes, alternating weekend delivery days with different brothers. The truck was always filled with cases of varying sizes of glass quarts of milk, and we had a milk carrier to carry the quarts and creams, and even eggs by the dozen. Every Saturday and Sunday I was up at 5 a.m. when the milkman would come pick me up to deliver the milk. I enjoyed working and meeting nice families who would give me a five cent coin as a tip. I was paid .50 cents a day and to me I felt like a rich 13 year old boy. The winter months were terrible because the milk bottle would freeze and the cream at the top of the quart would lift the cap off the quart. We had to keep a heavy blanket on everything to help keep the milk from freezing. In the summer months we had to chip ice blocks with an ice pick and spread the ice on the cases of milk to keep everything cold. I can't recall anyone using cuss words when I delivered milk. What I did hear was "we don't want to hear foul language, and if we do, we will wash your mouth out with soap."

During the weekend nights I shined shoes from 6 p.m. to 10 p.m. with a little shoe shine box I built. I had an old leather belt attached to the shoe shine box so that it was easy to carry up on the corner of the street I lived on. In those days, a shine cost .10 cents. I would earn a dollar, which included tips. I also sold newspapers at the same corner earning and additional .40 cents for the evening, which also included the tip. In that era, daily newspapers sold for three cents apiece, and if you were lucky you may have received a two cent tip. I was so proud running home and telling my mother how much I had earned for the evening.

Back then even the bread man would deliver fresh Italian 'Roma' bread to homes, and the cost was ten cents a loaf, which was a lot of money - not only for my parents but also the neighbors - who would complain on how prices were going wild. There were also the unforgettable ice cream trucks that drove up and down the streets ringing a distinguishable bell - loud and clear - for those of us who could afford a nickel or a dime.

As time went on the ice cream trucks in our neighborhood were replaced by the Pony Express Ice Cream, which was named for Ponies [Horse] that would pull a small wagon with a refridgerator and an umbrella to keep the driver from rain or sun. I applied for the job for $1.00 a day and - a free ice cream. I took the job because I knew I would enjoy the pony, who was called Spud.

Believe it or not, the use of ponies to sell ice cream became a big hit with everyone, because everyone who bought ice cream wanted to pet the pony. We were allowed to take on riders to sit in the wagon while the pony pulled the wagon. Those summers of pony driven wagons, as I remember them, became more popular than a regular ice cream truck.

"Hey! Uncle Louie It's snowing!"

In the late 1940's, my Grand Uncle Louie came from Italy to live at my parent's home and shared a bedroom with yours truly and my three brothers. From the eyes of a 12 year old boy [me] seeing Uncle Louie standing, he appeared as a giant of a tall man. Looking back I often wondered how all four people could fit in one small bedroom? Me and my two brothers shared one big bed, and there was a small single bed for Uncle Louie to sleep in. Can you imagine three boys and an adult sharing one bedroom? There was one small closet, just enough to store a few shirts and pants for the four of us. When anyone opened the closet door, it had the worse spooky squeaky sounding that scared the pants off of anyone who was not aware of it. We used to tie a string around the closet door knob and when Uncle Louie was ready to sleep, one of us boys would pull the door open slowly causing that real spooky sound and it made Uncle Louie become angry. In Italian he would yell out, "get that darn ghost out of that closet, and go to sleep!"

Back in those days we had furnaces and kitchen stoves that burned coal. Gas heat and oil heat were not much in use. Winters were dreadful, especially when folks would go to bed and pile blankets and coats on top just to keep warm during the night. Winters were very cold in the New England States and snow blizzards were a misery for those of us who had to shovel the snow off the sidewalks and walkways and steps that lead to the house. If you had three feet of snow loaded on your sidewalk, it had to be shoveled by hand, because in those days there were no snow blowers, mostly because no one could afford to buy one. It took four brothers and our father spending hours of hard labor removing the white stuff.

I remember my father going back into the house with anger to call Uncle Louie from his bedroom on the second floor to come help us remove the snow. Pop yelled in anger with a loud voice at the bottom of the stairs: "Uncle Louie come and help us remove the snow." Within a few seconds or so, Uncle Louie responded back: "whoever put it there, let him take it away." My father shook his head walking away in frustration, and before he came out to the side walk, he was laughing, and we didn't know what he was laughing about until he told us about Louie's response, and we all broke out laughing.

During the summers, Uncle Louie worked on a farm plowing the soil with the use of a horse named Tom who didn't understand English. Before the horse was taken out of the barn and the plow was attached, Tom would not leave the barn unless Uncle Louie put Tom's special top hat on him to keep the sun off his head.

I was not aware this horse only understood Italian. I would often pet Tom and talk to him, not knowing he didn't understand what I was saying until one day Uncle Louie asked me in Italian what I was saying to Tom. I had told Uncle Louie I was telling the horse how nice he is. Uncle Louie responded in Italian "Tom only understands Italian not English." I was so embarrassed that I made a fool of myself. But how was I to know the horse didn't understand English?

My Trombone

In my younger teens I once asked my father what he thought about someone in the family going into show business. Not knowing what show business was, he asked me "whatas disa showbis sell? Can yous eat disa for dinners and make a sandwich? Whats stores can you buys disa?" I asked myself, how in blazes can I explain 'show business' to my pop without getting an off the wall remark. One of my favorite instruments was the sound of a stand-up bass, which I use to mimic the sound of a bass and a trombone in the house. As a matter of fact I built a wooden trombone made with a long stick and a flat piece of wood to make it look somewhat like a trombone. I used to walk in or out of the house making the sound of a stand- up bass, or blasting out my trombone sound, which drove Pop insane with either sound, and he used to yell out; "takea dat stupid musica machine out of disa housa" and no play it in disa housea?' I remember walking through the kitchen making the sound of a trombone with my hand trombone piece of wood. The sound I created was done with my lips closed, and it about drove Pop out of his mind with anger. I remember my brothers telling me "you're driving the poor man insane with the bass and noisy trombone." For years, until I became an adult, the bass and trombone sounds always came with me into the house.

As a teen I recal the wind-up 'Victrola' that had to be cranked up to play records. We would play songs by Italian singers. I was barred from the use of playing that old- time machine because I used to slow it down to make the sound of an old bass singer. It was just a terrible sound that drove everyone away from that room. That same machine was given away due to the noise I was creating from it. Today it's nostalgic to buy them and considered a decorative antique. Most of them still work. As a matter of fact, my good friend Ron Della Chiesa owns one which he played several times for me when visiting him in Boston, and I have to admit the sound is superb, and each time a record is played, a new needle is installed to obtain the best sound.

"I Can Fortell The Future, I can predict coming events," says the gypsy, in a scene from "Girls, Girls, Girls" which was played by Frank E. Dee - left, as Dick Danielson, M.C. has his future told. The musical premiered on March 6th 1974 at the Bull In Shirley, Mass., one of the most unique dinner theaters in the state of Massachusetts. Photo taken March 4, 1974.

My days as a model for a local cothing store.

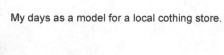

This is me singing as "Sinatra" and "Buddy Clark."

Magical Garage Door "Please God Open?"

In the early 1970's I was still drinking booze, however, I was a careful driver, but that was no excuse to drive while drinking." I had another Uncle who lived in a glass of so -called booze. It was a summer season and another Uncle was coming to visit my father and relatives. They called him Uncle Roberto. His father always told him he took after Uncle Roberto, because he was always doing things that were humorous or saying foolish things. My father was the type of person who didn't have time for humor. He was always a man who had to keep busy without taking time to laugh now and then. However I was looking forward to spending some time with my good ole Uncle Roberto, "because we both enjoyed drinking and laughter."

"Uncle Roberto never saw or knew anything about automatic garage doors. Back then automatic garage doors were the new in-thing, and it was wonderful because one did not have to get out of their vehicle to open the heavy garage door by hand, which was a difficult job. Truly it was a remarkable blessing to be able to stay in your car and open the door with a small remote. I remember most folks that owned a car kept their car in the house garage that had the installed automated garage door which opened with a remote opener. Most folks kept the remote opener in the car and another in the house.

"My old fashioned older relatives were not aware of new tools or automatic doors opening with a remote. When I took my Uncle to a rental home, at the time I was living in the suburbs, my uncle wanted to see the house and the room he would sleep in, as he was my guest. My father was quick to comment that being in a car driving 20 minutes was like a long drive from his home, and he would make a comment; 'If you go to ride in my son's car, you better pack a lunch because it takes 20 minutes to get to his home.' As for the old timers of my family, they were very negative when it came to spending time riding in a car for any length of time even if it was a 10 minute drive. You could always be certain to hear, 'are we almost there?'

As I approached the house with my Uncle, the garage door-was closed. I knew I was going to have some good clean fun with my Uncle - who was not aware of my plan. I parked the car in front of the door and concealed the remote, and I yelled out in a loud voice; "GOD PLEASE OPEN THE DOOR FOR UNCLE RO-BERTO!" Slowly the garage door began rising, and Uncle Roberto yelled out "Oh, No. How can this be?" I was holding back laughter as I watched Uncle Roberto clasp his hands as if he was to say a prayer. He was flabbergasted with emotion and somewhat fearful. He asked me if he could ask God to close and open the garage door. I told him to stand in front of the garage door and ask God in a humble way "please God close the garage door and then open the garage door." Uncle Roberto stood in front of the garage door pleading--- "please God close the door and then open the door." I kept the remote in my pocket and looked at Uncle Roberto who had an unusual look on his face. I told him, the reason why God did not close or open the door was because he didn't say; "please close the door, and please open the door." Still the door stood open. Finally Uncle Roberto yelled out to the door "the heck with you, stay open!" And that's when I closed the door, and showed him the remote. Talk about an uncle who was angry at a door that wouldn't open or shut for him."

Growing Up Italian In America

As we grow older our memory bank expands. We remember the past so we may realize who we are today.

I remember growing up Italian with my immigrant Ma and Pa. It seemed to me in those days people were more filled with love and compassion towards one-another. I think about my folks, and wishing they were still alive, I remember how hard they worked to raise a family with six kids.

The families of yesteryear were more family-oriented and had decent values. They immigrated to America for freedom and opportunity. They worked and they slaved; they took menial jobs usually offered to most immigrants. They dreamed not only for themselves, but for their children.

My parents cared for their children, and to some degree were strict and they couldn't speak English well, so as a youngster I felt foolishly ashamed. However, now, looking through a new pair of rose colored glasses I experienced maturity. I can kick myself for ever thinking that way.They really did the best they could to raise a large family. Our table was always laden with homemade pasta and other good food. My folks never stood in a bread line. They were too proud. Most American families in those depression days existed on peanut butter and jelly. I never saw peanut butter in our house. My parents classified it as junk food."

When I went to school my mother would make a large Italian sandwich, composed of a variety of cold cuts and along with some fruit, whe put it in a paper bag. I would feel ashamed to take out those eight-inch long sandwiches. But when I saw what other kids had for lunch, I always desired their sandwiches because they had peanut butter on two thin slices of "Wonder Bread." The other kids would drool at my "Hoagie," and I would swap for one of theirs. At that time I thought they were eating better than me, because they had peanut butter and I didn't.

I was even embarrassed by those large Italian sandwiches composed of peppers and eggs with onions and mushrooms wrapped in an old paper bag. After all, who could afford the fancy lunch bags available today. What embarrassed me was that the lunch bag was usually stained with olive oil. Yes, I felt ashamed to carry my own lunch bag that my mother worked so hard to prepare for me.

The cold cuts and cheese that Italians consumed were always imported. You never saw baloney or hot-dogs in an Italian household. What we did have were homemade Italian sausages - the Cadillac of the sausage. While most Americans were eating hot dogs and beans on a Saturday night, we were devouring steaks that my Pa would barbecue over red hot coals in the furnace, or sausages and thick pork chops fried in an old black cast iron frying pan steeped in olive oil with potatoes and onions, and there was always homemade wine and cake. The great quantities of food we consumed then are not considered healthful today. Too much cholesterol, too many calories. Nobody bothers to bake at home anymore. No time, and where it may seem most Americans eat to survive, Italians enjoy a romance with their food."

One day, when I was about eight, my neighbor gave me-some saltine crackers spread with peanut butter. It was the first time I ever tasted this sticky stuff that could clung to the roof of my mouth. With my two front teeth missing. I would pronounce peanut butter as feenat futter. I loved the stuff, so I ran back home yelling, 'Ma, Ma.' She was scrubbing floors that day, and I said to her, "Ma, buy me some feenat futter.' Boy did I love that creamy stuff.

The next day my Ma went to Tony's Italian Store and asked for feenat futter. The Italian owner, who couldn't speak English too well, said, "whata isa thisa thinga feenat futter."

After my neighbor translated, that was the first time peanut butter came into my house. My Pa would call it in Italian, "baby crap." He would never eat it or wanted to see it on the table, until years later. Then I learned about a new cheese that had holes in it named Swiss Cheese. It was new to me because I had never tasted it. So one day I did and liked it. I asked Ma to get a pound and she did. When I unwrapped the package and saw all the holes in it, I asked Ma, is this a full pound? There's too many holes in this cheese," I said. 'You were gyped on the weight.' Ma then angrily went back to Tony's store and complained to the Italian clerk, "with all those holes, it can't possibly weigh a pound.' "

Amazed, the poor clerk weighed the cheese and the old

scale pointed to more than a pound. Shaking his head, he asked what made her think she was getting ripped off. When she said, 'my son, said the cheese had too many holes," he replied, 'Thata sona of yours hasa holes in his head.'"

Today, Frankie confides "This stupid 'hole in the head' realizes he had the best parents in the world. " My only regret is that my children, and those to come have been cheated out of knowing a wonderful piece of their heritage – their grandparents and great-grandparents."

Growing Up Italian In America Is From Frank De Simone's True Humorous Italian Stories, which Has Appeared In Magazines and many Newspapers through columnist Joe Curreri.

Me and my Dad

And Yes... God Bless America!

    I often wonder that if the popular singer Kate Smith was alive and still singing Irving Berlin's immortal anthem "God Bless America" would the ACLU have stopped her from singing "God Bless America?" I recall the phrases Merry Christmas and God bless you were automatically accepted by all Americans.

    Which leads me to the topic of prayer. Prayer is powerful and it saves the lives of recovering alcoholics. Prayer saves family togetherness. Prayer brings peace for those who pray! Prayer helps people live a clean spiritual life style. Prayer helps the alcoholic and the drug addicts to become free from their addictions!

    The disgraceful organization, who wants public prayer removed, project their views as though they are against anything and everything that may pertain to the mention of prayer or God! And the United States Congress is just as bad, for being puppets dangling under the strings of the ACLU, and voting not to pass

the prayer amendment for our schools!   Back in 1941, when our American servicemen were called to go to war to defeat Germany and Japan, the American people, and foreign allies and all students in our American schools were asked to pray for our boys to return home safely and for our country to be at peace!? We were so proud to be able to pray for the support of our men and women in uniform, and for our country to be at peace!

I remember when the popular parades of the late 1940's and early 50's were attended by parents and their children, and when the American Flag passed on by all of us who were watching the parade, all the men took off their hats and placed them over their hearts, and adult ladies put their hand over their hearts as well in due respect of our beautiful American flag. We were all so proud of our American flag and our men and women who were serving in the armed forces to protect our freedom. And yes…Kate Smith singing "God Bless America!"

Today, Kate Smith can be heard singing "God Bless America" at every New York Yankees baseball game during the 7th inning break at Yankee Stadium - probably heard in person by 40,000 attendees and millions all over the world.

Do You Recall The Real 1940'S And 50'S?

If you can remember
When abortions were not
When family values came first
When riots were unthinkable
When you left front doors open
When socialism was a dirty word
When ghettos were neighborhoods
When our flag was a sacred symbol
When criminals actually went to jail
When we trusted God, and not politicians
When you weren't afraid to go out at night
When taxes were only a necessary nuisance
When a boy was a boy, and dressed like one
When a girl was a girl, and dressed like one
When the poor were too proud to take charity
When the clergy actually talked about religion
When clerks, and repairmen tried to please you
When college kids swallowed goldfish, not acid
When songs had a tune, and the words made sense
When young fellows tried to join the Army or Navy
When people knew what the Fourth of July stood for
When you never dreamed our country could ever lose
When a Sunday drive was a pleasant trip, not an ordeal
When you bragged about your hometown, and home state
When everybody didn't feel entitled to a college education
When people expected less, and valued what they had more
When politicians proclaimed their patriotism, and meant it
When everybody knew the difference between right and wrong
When things weren't perfect—but you never expected them to be
When you weren't made to feel guilty for enjoying dialect comedy
When our government stood up for Americans, anywhere in the world
When you knew that the law would be enforced, and your safety protected
When you considered yourself lucky to have a good job, and proud to have it
When the law meant justice, and you felt a shiver of awe at sight of a policeman
When you weren't embarrassed to say that this is the best country in the world
When America was a land filled with brave, proud, confident, hardworking people
This Was The America We All Remembered

God Bless America

I RECALL

Meeting Earle Tuttle

Meeting Publisher Earle W. Tuttle

If one is to drink alcoholically, like I did night and day, I can be truthful in admitting that I died mentally, physically, and spiritually. Because the only time I called out for God's help, was when I was into the shakes and vomiting. And that is when I called out for God's help, saying; "God if you help me to stop shaking and vomiting, I will not drink anymore." After years of sobriety with God as my wonderful master, I stop to think of those days making such dumb promises to God, and I shake my head thinking how stupid that statement was to promise God something He already knew - I would never keep my promise to stop drinking. But for some reason or other the Good Lord had plans.

As a young boy I always enjoyed writing little stories and poems for my own enjoyment, and also into adulthood. I always felt there was some type of force watching over me, simply because I wanted to be some kind of writer. I thought to myself. "You quit school at 16 years of age, and you're lucky if you can write your own name, let alone become a writer." However, the thought kept haunting me to try to look for a part time writer's job. But who and what was I going to write about? And who is going to hire such

a fool that didn't go to school? So, arguing with myself, I quit the thought of writing and went to work for Raytheon Company as a sheet metal worker on a second shift earning $1.50 an hour plus 5% percent more money for working on a second shift, with good medical benefits and vacation time. After all, being married and my home came first.

In our new housing development where I was living, free advertisements and newsy items would be deliv-

ered to all the homes (including free newspapers). I received a free copy of the local weekly newspaper called the News Enterprise which ran an ad "looking for part time reporter and sales person, to apply to publisher Earle W. Tuttle at the Beacon Publishing Company in Acton. Mass. I look back in the 1960's when I was living in a small town named Hudson, Mass., and at that time I was married. The thought kept coming to mind "we can always use extra money to pay our bills."

My interview was held on a Thursday morning at the Beacon Publishing Company which was located on the first floor of a big old building, and upon entering, the Secretary took my name and told me to sit and wait to be called by Mr. Tuttle. Within a few minutes I was taken into Mr. Tuttle's office and introduced to a 6 ½ foot tall man, who asked me to sit for my interview. He was a very kind soft spoken gentleman who asked what newspaper I worked at. I told him; "your advertisement did not ask for an experienced person. I did not have any experience working for newspapers at all." He asked me to sit at his typewriter and type a message from a piece of typewritten paper that he handed me. I was so nervous plinking and planking on those typewriter keys (at a much slower pace than any other human being). He quickly stated; "and you don't know how to type either right?" I got up from his typewriter and was ready to leave telling him I needed a part time job because of having two children and a wife and a house payment.

Mr. Tuttle was kind enough to offer me a part time job during the days in the printing department making up pages and ads and helping the pressmen when the newspapers were printed. In those years there was no such thing as "OFFSET PRINTING" and paper page make-up. In the meantime I was earning 15 hours part time, working alongside Mr. Tuttle doing page make up and proof reading and hot typesetting for the page make-up. Working alongside Earle was very enjoyable, and off hours he taught me how to type. Soon after, he gave me a typewriter to take home to use and learn how to write articles. I still ask myself today "where do you find a boss who goes all out to help your dream become a reality?" Later on I found out Mr. Tuttle was a very considerate spiritual man who helped poor people through his annual Christmas Santa Fund sponsored by the publications of his newspapers.

Sitting from the left Earle W. Tuttle former owner of The Beacon Publications of Weeklies Newspapers and Shoppers announces Frank E. Dee To Be The Manager and Editor Of The New 'TOWNE TALK' Shoppers in 1975; In The background are the Advertising sales men for the shoppers and newspapers.

While I was still employed with the Raytheon company working on the second 4 to 12 midnight shift, the company was beginning to cut back on employees, mostly employees with seniority who had the opportunity to be transferred to other long distance Raytheon plants, or go on layoff to collect unemployment/social security checks. Looking back, I was never one to sit and allow grass to grow under my feet. I learned from my father who always told us, "if you want something done, get off your rear and do it yourself, otherwise it won't be done." I was an individual who always liked working, because I had bills to pay and a family to support. And an unemployment check of 40 bucks a week wouldn't put enough bread and butter on the kitchen table to feed a family of four. Being an alcoholic they always managed to have enough money to buy a bottle of whiskey and in those days of the 60's a fifth of cheap booze sold for about three dollars.

I didn't know what I was going to do for a full time job. I didn't consider working full time for Mr. Tuttle, because I assumed my job working for him was always going to be a part time job. Earle was also a 'Doer' and got things done. I had learned a lot about making up ads and page make-up, and setting type into pages and proof reading and performing the corrections through this wonderful man who had the patience of 'Job' as he used to say. I didn't know what Earle meant when he said the 'patience of Job'. I thought he was talking about working on a 'job'. After all I came from the streets and wasn't too bright or well versed in the 'King's English.' Mr. Tuttle explained what the patience of Job meant. He addressed me as "Frank meboy, Job was from the Bible. He had patience, and ability to remain patient and do what you think you should do despite having many problems, to always do good things." I never forgot what he taught me about 'The Patience of Job.'

When I found out I was going to be laid off from my Raytheon Job, he was quick to ask me to go to work for the Beacon Publications, and at that time he had seven weekly papers one of which was 'The News Enterprise' located where I lived in Hudson, Mass. which was 3 or 4 miles from the Beacon plant. Mr. Tuttle called me into his office and told me to close the door behind me as he wanted to make a wonderful financial offer of $200.00 dollars a week, plus $37.00 dollars for gas and expenses, and of course health and medical coverage for my whole family. Plus two weeks vacation every year and a few holidays off. When I heard the offer I was ready to cry. Because $200.00 dollars a week was like a million dollars in the early 1960's, plus all the wonderful benefits he offered. I was kind of in a state of shock looking at Mr. Tuttle, and asking him "are you really serious?" I just could not believe the offer of a salary of $200 dollars a week.

I was deeply honored to have been employed as a manager of the News Enterprise weekly paper. My job was selling advertisements for the paper, and designing ads for customers and writing a political column titled "FOOTLOOSE", and a social column entitled "Our People". It was a delight being in the new plant, with new offset presses and computers to set the type. Then on Tuesday nights I laid out the 14 to 16 paper pagers and filled them with newsy and social articles and pasted them in the pages, and they were printed on a Wednesday morning, then I delivered them to stores and sports clubs. I truly earned my keep, and I loved my job. I honesty did not know why Earle Tuttle put up with my drinking. He could smell it when I walked into the new plant. I never missed work. I put that man through a lot of hurt. As months went into years I began an annual 'Dinner Dance' entitled "Welcome To Our Spring Dinner Dance," sponsored by the News Enterprise. Tickets sold for $5.00 for an all you can eat hot buffet. Of course there was a bar set up, from the 'Italian American Club.' The dances were always sold out and a lot of the local politicians showed up. Running a yearly dinner dance was a good way to gain new subscribers to the Enterprise. Earle was my biggest supporter.

Any employees working at the Beacon Publications whether they be a printer or page lay-out person or advertising making up artist, you could be 100 percent sure that you would never hear any foul language uttered in that plant.

In those years working for Beacon Publications, and managing one of the weekly newspapers, my drinking became worse. I was sneaking my drinking during the day and evenings. I always made sure I had breath Lozenges to eliminate the booze breath odor. And taking breath lozenges was a joke as people could still smell the booze breath. There wasn't a day gone by that Mr. Tuttle would walk up to me and take a deep breath and shake his head, and walk away from me, but never said anything. In the meantime my marriage was coming to an end and finally ended in divorce. After all, how can a husband be running around the pubs putting booze first before a marriage and coming home late at night half smashed and expect to keep a marriage together. The power of booze can destroy life, friendships, and marriages! Trust me, it's the truth!

Earle Tuttle was a very spiritual human being, who helped the poor and those in need. I thought to myself, please to try 'putting the plug in the jug' as they use to say. I did stay off the booze for about a year and decided to try getting into musical plays in the

"MUSICAL COMEDY MAN", had its smash opening this past Wednesday night at THE BULL RUNN in Shirley, Mass. Celebrating the opening are cast members of the Sawtelle Singers. From the left: Bill Wheeler, Laurie Lynch, Tammy Grimes, and Frank DeSimone.

evenings at the popular 'BULL RUN DINNER THEATER' in Shirley, Mass. I lucked out doing an audition and began rehearsals for the musical titled; 'Winter Wonderland'. Doing shows at the Bull Run, was a labor of love with no pay, just enjoyment. Staying busy got me away from, as they called it 'Johnny Barleycorn' [booze]. I continued doing a follow up show entitled; 'Girls, Girls, Girls'. I just wanted to remain busy and sober, and staying busy did keep me sober. I could tell Earle Tuttle was very proud of my staying off the sauce. During the day at work I stayed as busy as I could and my life became more manageable without drinking. It was nice feeling healthy and happier and a funnier me. Every morning I attended work extra-early waiting for Mr. Tuttle to show up, and he always expected my greetings. Earle was always into exercising, or playing golf and even or climbing mountains. He was a person who believed eating correctly and exercising, and on top of taking good care of his health, he was also very spiritual.

One morning I hid from his good morning greetings to. He asked the receptionist if I was in the plant. She answered 'yes' so Mr. Tuttle went from office to office calling my name. "Where in blazes are you?" I had hid under his desk and shouted out in a low sound voice; "I'm over here?" He walked up and down the hallways asking where was I.. "I'm in your office" was my response. When he came into his office I crawled out from under his desk. He never laughed so hard. There was always good clean humor, and my being sober really made me feel better. The only thing he didn't like was my smoking cigarettes. He pulled me aside and said; "Those things will kill you, and I'll bet you have a hard time breathing." Of course my answer was negative. He suggested we do a running race around the building at 12 noon. Sure enough the offices and even the back shop pressmen turned off the presses to see a race, strange as it seemed all the back shop employees were cheering me on, and of course the office employees were supporting Mr. Tuttle. The race began from the front office parking lot. There was only one way I could beat Mr. Tuttle in this race, after all the man was six feet six inches tall and I being five feet ten inches, what was my chance of winning this race. Well, making him laugh while running may help. And laugh we both did and he did win by a few feet. What a round of cheers we received from the company employees. Working for Earle W. Tuttle was one of the best jobs I ever had. He owned a beautiful home on a five acre estate with a private road leading to the home. He enjoyed his pool, his tennis court and his gazebo, and of course he loved playing his piano.

A few years later I decided I wanted to get remarried with Earle being the best man. The wedding reception was to be held on his estate. I recall helping Earle setting up decorations for the

PPER — JUNE 10, 1974

* SAWTELLE SINGERS A MUST *

"Musical Comedy Man" Superb Musical Show

Shirley Mass;;

It was a smash opening for the SAWTELLE SINGERS, Wednesday night, as the talented group returned to the boards of the Bull Run dinner theater, to pay tribute to George M. Cohan, in "Musical Comedy Man"....From the opening number, "All Aboard For Broadway", to the closing of "Your A Grand Old Flag", had the audience keeping time with their applause....Much credit is

due to the theater director Don Lussier, who is the musical genius of the fame dinner theater....The Sawtelle Singers prove this in the new musical, which will be staged every Wednesday and Thursday nights in the month of June....In July "Musical Comedy Man", will switch over to Friday and Saturday nights...."Musical Comedy Man" is a sparkling moving musical, full of life and

zest, and class....It's a musical that the whole family will enjoy namely at these perplexing times....To list a few of the George M. Cohan standards in the musical are: Give My Regards to Broadway, So Long Mary, Over There, Your a Grand Old Flag, Twentieth Century Love, Musical Comedy Man, Yankee Doodle Dandy, Only Forty-Five Minutes from Broadway, Harrigan....A small cover charge is well worth the good evening at the Bull Run...Don't miss the SAWTELLE SINGERS in "Musical Comedy Man"...

reception. He was on a ladder hanging decorations. I never forgot him looking down from the ladder and saying "This marriage will not work." Six months later it did end, through my going back to drinking.

I can never forget this wonderful, caring man who was always there trying to help me, and for other who needed help. Earle Tuttle was always there for everyone.

DeSimone Says He Is Concerned For Elderly

Frank DeSimone, a candidate for the five year term on the Hudson Housing Authority, comments in a statement issued today, that concern for housing for the elderly of the town caused him to seek the post.

"I've been a resident of Hudson for the past 10 years", he said, "and during the past couple of years, I've become increasingly concerned with the problems that our elderly citizens have just making ends meet. I've always been interested in helping our senior citizens cope with their problems. One of the biggest that I have found, is decent, comfortable housing that they can afford on their fixed income. To help them is the reason I'm running for Housing Authority.

Besides the problems of housing for our senior citizens, we have the problem of housing for low and moderate income families. Where can they reside at reasonable rents? How about young people just getting married; where will they live

FRANK DeSIMONE, candidate for a five year term on the Housing Authority.

Maybe we should look into this problem too and try to solve it.

If you were to ask me if I had all the answers I'd have to tell you honestly that I don't and any candidate who tells you that he's got all the answers, is talking through his hat. No one can really understand the

DeSimone Says He Is Concerned For Elderly

Continued from page 1

workings of a board until he's elected to it. No one is born into an office; we must all learn by experience.

I would like to be elected to the Housing Authority and with your vote on April 3, I can become a member of that board. All I can promise you is that I'll do my best to work towards a solution to the housing problems of all the citizens of Hudson."

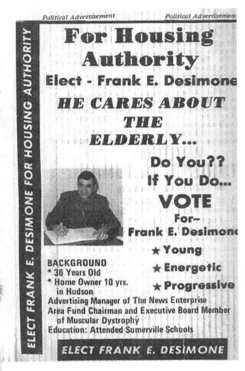

Frankie Dee

A special sketch of yours truly was used for promoting the Frankie Dee Shows over WHET back in 1978. Thanks be to my news publisher boss Earle W. Tuttle owner of the Beacon Publications who backed my shows. He was one of the best bosses and best friend I have ever met and worked for. Thank you Earle for all you did for me. Mr. Earle W. Tuttle also stood behind Bill Marlowe for advertising Earle's weekly newspapers and printing for customers.

I RECALL

American Liberty News

Thanks To American Liberty News Writers

After my first heart attack in my 4th year of sobriety it seemed that everything I did always turned out to be a miracle and at this time I decided to quit my job from a printing company at the age of 54 and to collect social security and Medicare due to my heart problem, where I was allowed to go on Social Security disability. At that time I wasn't aware of what I was going to do, because I was one who always worked and stayed active, be it on a job or working in my garden. However I was getting bored, because I wanted to do something different, I wasn't one - as the saying goes - to allow grass to grow under my feet. Meanwhile I remained active by starting up an alcoholic recovery meeting clinic to help women, men and young teens get sober. I have to be totally honest and say how blessed I have been by my elder peers in the program who always taught me Godly concepts that helped me to live a good clean life without booze. These words from my good friends who taught me the spiritual way of living life daily by faith, were 100% right. They said "we came to believe in God without any problem, because turning our life over to the care of God brought daily miracles and you found out that prayer is the world's greatest wireless connection, and through God, numerous wonders have happened."

Meanwhile, during the day I wanted to stay busy and learn about computers, which back in the 1980's, were only just beginning to become popular in homes. I had to learn how to start to use the magical electric keyboard and learn a new way of typing, which was a lot different than typing on an old typewriter. I had some good friends who attended my meetings and took me to a computer company where they manufactured new computers and printers. At that time I thought I was going to have a heart attack when they told me the price of this unit, [the computer] was about $800.00 for the computer and $400 for the printer, and don't forget in that era computers were quite big and bulky machines, and the computer monitor was about $300.00. Also back then, the internet was just becoming popular. I mean, who in blazes heard of a computer and the internet, after all, I came from an era where computers were known as large floor machines. And who really knew anything about the internet at that time? I was blessed to have good friends teach me how to use a computer and how to make up pages on the internet to create websites.

I was very fortunate to meet a wonderful Christian gentleman named Mike Roberts from Virginia who was a web site designer and who owned his own company Old Dominion Internet Solutions. Mike was one of the best website creators, who went all out to help me to design own website "Golden Music Memories of Yester-year." He made it all happen. Negative people told me it couldn't be done, including a woman telling me the title was too long and it won't work. Well today in the year of 2015 the web site is still up and running and has became an award winning website. And so much for the negative people who kept telling me "It can't be done." Thanks be to God, it was accomplished.

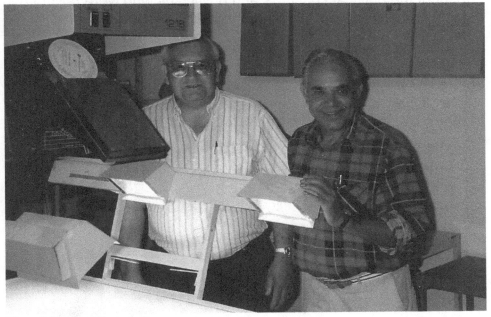

Warren Marsh and Me

I have always been one who enjoyed staying busy and creating little projects and I still had a desire to create newsy news to add to my message forums on Gmmy websites. I was honored to have received a phone call from a gentleman who owned a print shop, his name was Warren Marsh who wanted to get together to create a monthly newsletter. We became wonderful partners. We created the newsletter titled 'American Liberty News' which was a conservative monthly news media in which we endorsed the tax-payers, and the Christian news against abortion. The partnership with Warren Marsh and yours truly was a wonderful relationship promoting God and the Christian way of living.

My job was to set the type for our monthly 28-30 page publication plus the page layout, which I did in my home offie, and then I would bring the pages to Warren's print shop - Orbit Printers. Once they were printed, I collated the pages and stapled them together. We used to print 150 newspapers filled with complete news and editorials. Once all the newspapers were printed I would take them to various news stores and liquor stores. At the time of our publication we had people who began to subscribe to our news paper for $20.00 for 12 monthly issues, and we really did not make money, it was something Warren and I both needed to do to get the message out about the political spenders and politicians who were raising our taxes, and of course we were 100 percent against abortion.

Some great writers contributed their columns to our American Liberty News - there was Bill Marlowe and Ron Della Chiesa, both popular Boston radio hosts, the popular news writer Paul Harvey, Charles Shows producer and cartoonist and author of Walt Disney's life, Jim Cornick, from Warner Brothers studio, and author/

Early 1990's: publishers of AMERICAN LIBERTY NEWS Frank E. Dee and Warren Marsh. A monthly conservative publication printed at warren's print shop Orbit Printers. Thank you Warren for the wonderful working years we shared. I was honored to have met and become a partner with Warren, who was a wonderful spiritual gentlemen and a close friend. We never had a bad word between us, only to the political spenders. God bless you Warren, I know your with God's angels in heaven.

writer Joe Curreri who donated his columns about the singers and film stars, and Terry Robinson who wrote about healthy exercising and food.

Warren Marsh was a wonderful spiritual man who treated me as though he was an elder brother. It was difficult visiting him in the hospital and knowing he was going to pass away. When I stop to think of those wonderful days working together, it brings tears to my eyes - what a great human being.

As I look back on those years of writing and the group of people who labored for our American Liberty News, I recall a good clean bunch of humorous men and that are now gone. God bless them all for being there and being a big part of American Liberty News.

AMERICAN Liberty

Volume-4 — Dedicated to the American Dream — Merry Christmas December-1992

Merry Christmas And A Happy New Year To All

America Is At War!
Against The Real Killer!
The National Deficit!

By Charles Shows

When America is threatened by any foreign country, large or small, our people immediately go on a full-time war footing. To protect America, we all join the army, navy, marines, air corps, or homefront soldiers. We quickly prepare to fight for our lives and for the American dream. We will fight and, if need be, die for our precious homeland!

Continued On Page-14-See America Is At War

It's Time To Call U-Haul...Or
Barbara, Start Baking The Cookies

Bye George! By Jim Cornick

From All indications, the majority of the voting populace was ready for a change and were willing to ignore rumors, lies, questionable lack of ethics, and yes, even some truths, involving the credibility, the patriotism, the experience, and the lack of moral conduct on the part of the New, Great White Hope, of 1600 Pennsylvania Blvd. But before we jump to conclusion and play into thought that "·~ best man won the race, let's review the comedies, ,,edies and drama which were presented to the audience of the United States, on the stage of The American Dream.

Continue On Page -5-See Hollywood Jim...

Social Security Warning!
System May Go Broke!!

By Charles Shows

If you are paying into Social Security—as most Americans are—you are in for a horrible surprise! Today, Social Security is a time bomb, ticking away until it will explode in our faces!

The present high Social Security taxes would and should be enough to give us our money back when we retire at 65 years of age, but it will not be there when we need it!

Continue On Page-15 See Social Security Warning!

A Time To Be Scared?

By Paul Harvey

Enough people enjoy being frightened to make Halloween significantly profitable.

Enough people enjoy being frightened so that any book alleging "the sky is falling" has a guaranteed market.

Those of us upon whom you depend to separate the real from the false alarms grow very skeptical of professional pessimists.

Continue On Page-13-See Paul Harvey

America's Best Columnist
-Paul Harvey-
Is A Monthly Feature in...
American Liberty Pages-10, 11, 13, 17, 26

'Then join hand in hand brave Americans all! By uniting we stand, by dividing we fall!'

American Liberty Editorials And Views

By Frank E Dee

In God We Trust	*-Dedicated To The American Dream-* *"Then join hand in hand, Americans all! By uniting we stand dividing we fall."* *"The ballot is stronger then the bullet."-Abraham Lincoln-May 19, 1856*	The Editorial Newsletter

An Open Letter To Santa Claus

Have A Cool Yule...   *By Frank E. Dee*   And A Happy First

Start **Thinking!**

Or We Will All Be...

Sinking!

By Frank E. Dee

Dear Santa:

Voters Will Continue To Moan And Groan

First of all, are you ready for what's been going on in this country? Please allow me to dump some newsy stuff your way. Santa, I really don't know why the voters voted Senator Boxer back into office, when they knew she was bouncing rubber checks, and her attendance has not been the greatest in Washington. Seems to me Santa we deserve the government we elect. We've heard the voters complain, moan and groan, and yet they voted Senator Boxer back into office. This Santa I'll never understand? However the elections are over with, and the voters put back the spendthrift, and the people will continue to moan and groan as the spending continues on with the likes of Boxer.

Bruce Herschenson A Better Choice

Santa, I think the voters really made a boo-boo by not voting in Bruce Herschensohn. For my money, He would have been a better Congressman. The man is honest, and believed that our government was overspending (as if we all didn't know) and I firmly believe that Bruce would have done more for the State of California, and his constituents. I also believe that there was a lot of dirty political garbage brought out on Bruce, that were total lies. For instance American Liberty News is delivered into a lot of Magazine stores. Does that make us porno freaks, just because we deliver American Liberty News where porno material is sold? So Bruce bought his news papers where porno garbage was being sold! Big Deal! That certainly doesn't make the man a kook on porno books, or whatever! How many times Santa, do people stop at any book store or magazine store that sells news papers, just to buy a paper? Does that label these people also porno readers? It certainly was dirty pool brought up that was uncalled for! What some people will do, just to get elected. Huh Santa?

For God's Sake...Keep God Alive!

Santa baby, lets hope that everyone in the United States supports the Boy Scouts by allowing the Boy Scouts to hire whom they please when they please, and to keep God in the Boy Scout Oath. You see Santa, Levi-Straus maker of Jeans has a problem with the use of God being used in the Boy Scout Oath, and not to forget Wells Fargo Bank as well, both are against the Scouts for not hiring homosexual scoutmasters. If we take God out of the Boy Scout Oath, then we should take out God in the courts, when people are sworn in. How about when a new Congressman is sworn in?? We watched Senator Diane Fienstien being sworn in on November 10, and as she concluded by holding up her right hand she said: "So help me God." Are they not sworn to oath under God? We already have allowed the courts to take prayer out of schools! What's next Churches? How about our currency? "In God We Trust." When it comes to money...Why is it that Levi-Straus and Wells Fargo Bank don't ask to take off "In God We Trust?" Hmmm!! Could it be that "Money talks, and B.S. walks."

Consumer's Pay High Prices At Food Stores

Santa, here's one of the best I've heard yet! Not too many of the common grocery shopper may know this. Did you know Santa that when a distribution company that supplies soft drinks or can foods to chain stores, they have to pay large sums of money for shelf space? On top of this, the stores continue to make a double profit. So if you folks wonder why some of your can good prices don't come down in price, perhaps a good letter to their cooperate headquarters could make a difference. Santa, I honestly don't think it's right that these chain stores charge a distributor for shelf space, then charge more for the product to the consumer. You and I!!

Continue On Page-16-See Dear Santa

> *Support Proposition 13. With A Donation The Taxpayers Friend*

American Liberty Editorials And Views

By Frank E Dee

In God We Trust	-Dedicated To The American Dream- "Then join hand in hand, Americans all! By uniting we stand dividing we fall." "The ballot is stronger then the bullet."-Abraham Lincoln-May 19, 1856	The Editorial Newsletter

Congress Gains, While Elders Pain!

Congress Is Sad, Pathetic, And A Disgrace To The American People On Fixed Income

By Frank E. Dee

While Congress continues to enjoy another 3.2 cost of living increase at our expense, the senior on fixed income, who depend on their Social Security check continue to reap the harvest of poverty.

The new $6,000 increase per year added to the congressmen present salary, $129,500 will now be $135,644. How sweet it is for them!

In a recent tour of FHP (a senior plan Medicare hospital facility), that covers healthcare for seniors, who can not afford regular hospital care or prescription drugs sold at regular drug stores, are finding it difficult to pay the fee of $5.00, for treatment at FHP, due to being on a fixed income Social Security check.

Do you honestly believe that the Congress and Senate know the pain that these elders are going through with healthcare? We think not! Do you think they care?

I have seen the crying of pain and the worry of faces that are filled with sadness and the worry look of these seniors, as they wonder how they can afford to even pay $5.00 for a visit, or $5.00 for a prescription.

In the mean time Congress continues to reap the harvest of pay increases while the seniors continue to go down the tubes of a no healthcare program. What a shame and disgrace!

American is one of the riches' countries in the world, yet, the government is always sending billions to other countries, and yet casting our own people into debt and not doing a damn thing about a healthcare program that all would benefit from it. What a disgrace! What kind of people do we have in this congress of ours, that allow our own people in these United states to be last instead of first?

You can rest assure that members of Congress and the Senate have the best benefits not only in a healthcare program, but they also end up with a fat pension at our expense!

It is high time that a march to Washington by "we the people" let these greedy careless politicians hear the people's cry of poverty, and that "we the people," be heard!

We must stop the Congress and the Senate from doing as they please! We have allowed them to spend, more and more of our tax dollars on benefits that is of their gain and not of ours! We can Stop the spenders, by voting them out, and making new laws that they will abide by "we the people." If it takes a good old "Boston Tea Party," then so be it!

No, Congressmen or Senate member is worth $135,644, plus all the benefits that go with this so called house of "spend as you go taxpayer's money."

We need to get the Congress and Senate off their butt, and put in a healthcare program and start spending money in this country by taking care of our own people first. It's simply called: "First Things First."

****

Start **Thinking!**

Or We Will All Be...

Sinking!

By Frank E. Dee

When Is Congress Going To Do Something About Healthcare??

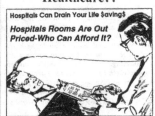

Hospitals Can Drain Your Life $aving$

Hospitals Rooms Are Out Priced-Who Can Afford It?

Support Proposition 13. With A Donation The Taxpayers Friend

AMERICAN Liberty

| Volume-3 | *Dedicated to the American Dream* | November-1992 |

We Need To Support Proposition 13

Politicians And Bureaucrats Still Trying To Push Proposition 13 Out And New Taxes In. HJTA Continues To Fight For Taxpayers

By Joel Fox, President
Howard Jarvis
Taxpayers Association

Dear Fellow Taxpayers, of California:

We won! On June 18 the United Supreme Court upheld the constitutionality of Proposition 13 by an 8-1 vote. Our victory was the result of a tough and extremely expensive four-year legal battle. We put forward a first-class defense of Proposition 13, and your generous support made it all possible.

Continue on page-16-See-Politicians and Bureaucrats still trying to push Proposition 13 out.

Hey, Big Spender!

By Paul Harvey

If you encounter your senator or congressman in person this campaign time, you are likely to be more respectful than he deserves.

You are entitled to greet him: "Hey, big spender!" Because most all members of both houses of Congress have sponsored or voted in favor of increased federal spending.

Seventy - three percent of senators and 85 percent of House members have proposed legislation that would result in a net federal spending increase of more than $5 billion.

continue On Page-20...See-"Big Spender"

This Article Has Been Written In The U.S.A. - By A Citizen Of The U.S.A.

By Jim Cornick

Looking into the abyss, of our country, over the past twelve years, I saw the abyss looking back at me, and asking. "What have you done for your country lately?" Over the past ten months, it has been my pleasure to share my views with the readers of the "Senior Truth Action News," and more recently with the "American Liberty News." These articles, I'm sure, at times appeared to be no more than, "bushing," but were actually an attempt to call attention for the issues which I feel Need to be addressed, if indeed "we the people" are to take our country back from a bureaucracy made up of professional "liars, cheats and thieves."

Continue On Page-5-See As Hollywood Jim Sees It.

Howdy, Suckers!

By Charles shows

Of course I know and you know none of our readers are suckers...but our insane Congress considers all taxpaying Americans to be suckers!

It would take a book the size of the Encyclopedia Brittainica to list all the horrible problems in our outdated, greedy, inept and cowardly Congress.

continue On Page-22-See-Howdy Suckers-*By Charles Shows*

Have A Safe And Happy Thanksgiving

'Then join hand in hand brave Americans all! By uniting we stand, by dividing we fall!'

I RECALL

Bill Marlowe - A Radio Great

A Special Salute To Bill Marlowe
From Massachusetts Broadcasters Hall Of Fame
At Massasoit Community College
Hall Of Fame: 2012

BILL MARLOWE

In the 1950's he introduced thousands of listeners to the growing body of work by Frank Sinatra. As one Marlowe fan put it, "It was as if Bill were an extension of Sinatra and a part of the whole performance"

1924-96: A Boston radio icon for much of his fifty year career, Bill was revered for his enthusiastic, emotional, and booming voice and his exceptional musical taste. A native of Boston's North End. Bill began his career at WCCM Lawrence, Mass, moving to WBZ where he championed the songs and singers of the Great American Songbook and jazz vocalists. In the later years, Bill was heard on WILD Radio Boston and WHET, Waltham. In the 1950's he introduced thousands of Listeners to the growing body of work by Frank Sinatra. As one Marlowe fan put it. "It was as if Bill were extension of Sinatra and a part the whole performance." He had close personal relationships with Ella Fitzgerald, Nat Cole, Sarah Vaughan, Duke Ellington, Sinatra, and countless others. Bill also was a connoisseur of good foods, and a critic, and one of the best salesmen in Broadcasting history, he personally tested the products of potential advertisers before agreeing to take them on and to this day is remembered for his emotional ads for a restaurant where "The meat falls off the bone!"

My Radio Mentor Bill Marlowe

Bill Marlowe Was Music's Best Friend

Thank You Bill For Being There For Me ...

I Love You Bill And Miss You

by Frank E. Dee

Bill Marlowe was born in the North End of the Italian section of Boston. He was a proud Italian, but had to change his name due to the era of time in the early 40's. He said: "If you were an Italian, radio management would not hire you."

Bill Marlowe was one of the rarest and most impeccable Radio Musical hosts, who ever sat behind a microphone, at any given radio station in the United States. He indeed was the "Voice" of radio. He touched so many people over his 55 years in radio with compassion, love and care. I named him: "The Baron of the Airwaves" and rightfully so. He was incredible! He was one of a kind and was loved by thousands, and thousands of friends. Yes, he truly was "King of the Radio Airwaves" in the New England States. Bill worked for numerous radio stations throughout the New England areas, including New York stations; WNEW, WCBS-FM, and WHN-FM, and in Florida at WMBM at Miami Beach. In the Boston area he worked at WORL-AM, WBZ-AM & FM, WRKO-AM, WILD-AM, WNTN-FM, WHET-AM, WLYN-AM and up to his untimely death he was at WRCA-AM, Stereo. His radio career began at the age of 9 years, when he made his radio debut reading a 'Hamlet Soliloquy,' on WEEI FM. He started his full time radio show at WCCM-AM in Lawrence, Massachusetts, in the 1940's. From that time on, he became a legend, who would not

Pen and Ink Drawing of Bill Marlowe

compromise in playing Rock 'N' Roll - what he called "trash."

Bill was the only radio personality in history who stood-up to radio management in keeping good MUSIC of the 30's, 40's, 50's alive on all his radio shows whatever station he may have been at. He refused to listen to management who tried to change his format to 'Rock 'N' Roll, or go with the flow of the other radio stations that would air 'Rock.' And yours truly can relate to that! Marlowe would tell management where to go. But compromise never! He said numerous times over his shows live: "I'd rather commit suicide than play Rock 'N' Roll. But it's expensive to be an aesthetic [person]. If I had played Rock 'N' Roll, I'd own 10 stations and be a multimillionaire, but can you be a prostitute? I can't." Bill was dedicated to his radio audience and he provided the music they loved most. He said so many a times "I love my country, but we have lost perspective musically. We live in a permissive society, and it's a shame. I play good music, and the other stuff to me is pure c-r-a-p." Even though the news media had a field day with what he said. He still stood his ground, and within time, the same news media who knocked him, praised him for sticking to what he believed. And that was always featuring the great bands, vocalists, lush plush songs and just plain good music.

Bill lit the way by playing good music - Jazz, Big Bands, and featuring such giants as Arthur Prysock, Nat Cole, Mel Torme, Al Martino, Tony Bennett, Mario Lanza, Frank Sinatra, and the 'Kitten' as he called her… "Dakota Staton", and he would introduce to his audience Diana Washington as: "Diana like in 'Dynamite' Washington." Marlowe had the charm, the charisma and the voice to match.

Bill would not accept any restaurant sponsors that he thought were not up to good standard. Before he would record commercials for restaurants, he would first go to the restaurant and dine, and if the restaurant's food didn't meet up to his standard of serving good food, he would not take them on as a sponsor. No matter how much money they would offer Bill to sponsor their restaurant. Bill was a connoisseur of good foods, and a critic of good wines. If the food was not up to par, or needed extra ingredients he would take the dish into the kitchen and show the chef what needed to be added.

Every Boston Restaurant proprietor knew him well. If you walked into a restaurant where Bill would be dining, you knew that Bill's personality cast a bright light that lit-up the room with his magical comical humor. Often times he would go into the kitchen no matter where he was dining and tell the chef how to cook certain dishes the way he liked, and when Marlowe promoted a restaurant or one of Boston's famous eateries over his radio shows, he had the magical gift of making your mouth water for the food he was promoting.

Often Bill would invite me to join him in one of the many Italian Restaurants that belonged to his sponsors, and when I would visit Boston every year, Bill and I always hooked up. He would say: "Let's go eat some good food. He loved to eat, and as we would be dining, I can remember him telling me, "Frankie, don't let the good music die, keep it alive, and do something with it on this new thing called the 'INTERNET.' Keep on promoting the Perry Como's, Al Martino's, and the Tony Bennett's, who have contributed so much to our society and to good music." I kept my word, and will always continue on and on as time permits me to do so.

Bill was proud to be an Italian, and he didn't care who knew it, or didn't know it, and he made sure he would mention it over his shows. He was an ardent fan of Frank Sinatra. He would also say, "nobody in the world - or in future generations to come - will ever have a set of pipes like Mario Lanza." He even got into a fight at one of the radio stations he was at in the 50's, with a colleague DJ at the same station who told Marlowe, "This guy stinks! He won't last." Bill sent the DJ to the floor and the press had a field day in tormenting Bill as the "Bad Boy of Radio." Bill was a gentle giant, but never allowed anyone to criticize the stars of his format.

Bill Marlowe became my radio mentor, my teacher. Had it not been for Bill I would have never become a D.J. Bill Marlowe was the one who opened the doors of radio for me at WHET-A.M. We both had our own separate radio shows, and we kept to the same format, and we never compromised. He never played down to the audience. He always continued to play the music he liked up until his passing on a Saturday July 21, 1996, and at that time the entire radio industry took a moment of silence to pay tribute to Bill Marlowe. Entertainment stars of all walks came to his funeral, or sent their condolences to a man who stood up alone to play the good sounds of music. Bill Marlowe was called the "Radio Personi-fication of the Rat Pack" by all the news media. He truly was one of a kind, and a tough act to follow.

Every Summer I would go back To Boston to visit family and friends, and "Billy" as we called him, would always invite me on his show as a guest. He would make reservations to dine out in an Italian Restaurant, and a special area was secured for his invited guests such as Ron Della Chiesa, of WGBH FM, and the manager of the North Shore Music Tent. Ron, Bill, and yours truly were real close friends, and Bill was Ron's mentor as well. Bill Marlowe was indeed a lovable, humorous guy with a heart as big as his six foot body.

Back in the early 1950's when nationwide disc jockeys were implicated in the popular radio payola scandal, Bill was one of the rare radio hosts who were far above being suspect. He was quoted in a 1974 interview in the Boston Papers "they knew no one was paying me to play Sarah Vaughn, Sinatra, Al Martino, Lanza, Da-kota Staton, Bennett, Jerry Vale and my buddy Errol Garner." Bill Marlowe was one who would never allow anyone to bribe him into promoting their recordings. He always said "don't take me for grant-ed, and I certainly will not take you for granted. When Bill passed on, his good friend talk show host Jerry Williams did a special eu-logy show of Bill's life. I have a copy of that tape, and it is the most remarkable dedication I have ever heard. It will bring tears to your eyes. To Jerry Williams I say, thank you, sir. No one could have expressed such warmth and feelings as Jerry did on his show.

It was Bill Marlowe who introduced me to Ron Della Chiesa, another giant of good music, from Station WGBH-FM and WPLM-FM. After Bill had passed away, Ron Della Chiesa took over his format playing the same good sounds that Bill always featured. You can hear Ron's shows at WPLM-FM on weekends and of course every morning on GMMY RADIO from 7:30 A.M. to 9:30 A.M. 6 days a week, what a way to start your day.

I was deeply honored that Bill's fiancée, Helen, called me to tell me that Bill Marlowe wanted me to have some of his taped shows. I often will pull out a memory tape of Bill's show, and listen to the beautiful artists who sang these great songs, and to quote Bill's famous saying "that would make one's goose bumps stand up like little tin soldiers."

I was deeply honored to have Bill Marlowe write articles in my American Liberty Newsletter for 8 years up until his passing. And he didn't spare the horses when it came time to write his col-umn about politicians or whoever. When Bill passed away Ron Della Chiesa took over the helm by writing about interesting show people and opera stars.

On Bill's 50th year in radio I was his surprise guest without him knowing I was going to be on his show. I presented him over the air a beautiful portrait of himself which was drawn by an artist

Frank E. Dee, Bill Marlowe Sax player star; Illinois Jacquet, photo taken at Monticello Night Club in Framingham, Mass where Illinois Jacquet appeared to a standing ovation audience. He was a close friend to Bill Marlowe and Bill invited me to be his guest.

friend, and a letter that was sent to me by Frank Sinatra, to be read in the presence of Bill, over the air. As I read Mr. Sinatra's letter, Bill had tears in his eyes. It was one of the most touching shows I have ever done, for a friend who I loved so dearly, and who truly deserved the accolades for all his years being dedicated to good music. If Bill was here with us today, he would have continued on and on with the same format by providing the best in music. On a special tribute from the staff of WRCA they dedicated "I DID IT MY WAY." And Bill Marlowe certainly did. I know for a fact that it Bill Marlowe were still alive, he would certainly be on GMMY RADIO daily.

Pesto Ala Bill Marlowe

Bon Appetito...With Love

I have always enjoyed homemade Italian cooking which I learned from my parents who were born in Italy and knew every homemade Italian recipe. When I moved to California I have often invited about 6 to 10 people to my home to enjoy my homemade Pasta, Italian meatballs and good old homemade Italian salad.

One of the greatest Italian recipes was passed on to me from my close Boston radio mentor, and close friend Mr. Bill Marlowe who really was a connoisseur of Italian food. I attended a number of Italian restaurants, by way of an invitation from Bill when I was living in Boston, and also while performing my radio show at WHET-AM. Bill was noted to dine in the best of restaurants, and he would never take on any restaurant as an advertiser for his shows just to make a buck, unless Bill went into the kitchen and tasted the food. If Bill thought the food was not up to his standards of good taste he would refuse the restaurant as an advertiser for his shows, and I know this to be a fact because I was always invited by Bill for a good Italian dinner in restaurants he promoted.

Bill would often chat about good recommendations of Italian homemade recipes and how to prepare an Italian dish to serve to invited guests at a dining room table at his home and properly set a table before serving. One thing I adored, when Bill would would say; "Don't allow grass to grow under your feet, get the job done nicely." Well, I always knew that, and I didn't have to be reminded about grass growing under my feet.

Listed is a copy of Bill Marlowe's recipe he had sent me some years ago to be published in the American Liberty News, for which Bill wrote monthly articles. I shall never forget this man and all he did for me. All of us who knew Bill, would often say "Bill is up in heaven cooking for all the angels and saints."

Pesto Ala Bill Marlowe Recipe

- 6-cups of basil [loosely packed]
- 1-cup Pignolli nuts
- 3-cloves of garlic
- 1-cup of Pecorino Romano cheese
- 1 ¼-cup of Italian olive oil - (Frankie, be sure to buy the best olive oil]
- Add juice of 1 lemon
- Sprinkle in a little black pepper

In a mix-master blender grind nuts thoroughly to a paste, and remove from container.

Place cleaned and dried (5 cups basil) into a mix-master or blender – grind fully, then add garlic, olive oil and cheese then grind and blend, for 30 seconds. Finally, add nuts [that are in paste form] and put machine on blend until all is mixed and can be poured into receptacles for future consumption. Pesto may be frozen.

When you defrost do not microwave it. Let it float in a bowl of hot water until it softens.

Frankie, enjoy and pass it along.

Bon Appetito ...With Love

Bill Marlowe

'Stop Already!' by Bill Marlowe

Some say we are relating to the great classic movies as still some of the best? The films of yesteryear had theme, thesis, and story-lines. The acting was superb, the music [background], was rending and befitting. Heart throbbing, dramatic or comedic, those films were classic from every aspect. Here's a list of some of the all time greats actors; Ollivier, Newton, Tracy, Gable, Barrymore, Davis, Garbo, Cagney, Bogart, Grant, Douglas, Stanwick, Hopkins and all the magnificent character actors and actresses. With the exception of a handful of motion pictures of today, most of these movies are weak, pitiful, violent, dirty, cheap and vile - the lowest of the low.

They are a disgrace to watch - and to be associated with America - for those who watch this garbage in other countries. Hollywood has become a disgrace and the pecuniary curses who are responsible for fostering this poop. What a sad documentary for our wonderful country and the youth who can't compare.

Whatever happened to the promises Hollywood collectively made to clean up their act and to cut down on violence and hostility? More bureaucratic baloney from the money makers. I saw a motion picture that sickened us all. It was obviously made to cater to an audience composed of morons or rather idiots. It was one of the worst pictures that was ever perpetrated on the human race. Before we witnessed the abomination, this horror, this inexplicable thing called "In the mouth of madness," we witnessed coming attractions. More violence, more killings, more maiming, more outrageous sex, and more filthy language. When does this filth stop? When will it be fought? Must we march on Washington? Me thinks money talks loud and clear again just like dope lives here openly and clearly. My frustration is heard by all and frequently on all my broadcasts because I'm mad as hell and sick of the system and all who are part of it because of the evil stinking blood buck.

This article above was written by the late great New England radio and TV host Bill Marlowe from Boston, who was my radio mentor. The article below appeared in our front page of American Liberty News issue on May 1995.

He chose the title above.

Backing up a bit to the year of 1995, I created the monthly newsletter American Liberty News, which was a political newsletter of 28 pages published and printed, with some of the best well known writers such as Paul Harvey, Bill Marlowe, Charles Shows, Terry Robinson, Joe Curreri, Yours Truly, Warren D. Marsh [my friend and printer and partner]. I took the liberty of setting the type at home and doing all the page make up  and then taking it to Warren's print shop to be printed and collated, and delivered to stores and mailed out to subscribers. To be 150 percent honest we didn't make a dime, it truly was a labor of love to get the word out about politicians - our goal was fighting against high taxes. After Bill Marlowe's passing on July 21 1996, Boston's popular radio host Ron Della Chesa took over writing about great singers and operas. I honestly had a hard time trying to forget Bill for all the good things he did for all who needed his help, and I for one never forgot him helping me to learn how to run radio equipment. Bill I miss you and so do all your friends and fans.

Dinning out - my visit to Boston from California. Bill Marlowe invited me and Lorraine Parretti, a big fan from Massachusetts, of Bill Marlowe (and my dear friend as teens growing up in my Boston years).

Boston Radio Days with Bill Marlowe

"Had it not been for Boston's popular radio disc jockey Bill Marlowe, who I had interviewed for an article about Bill's life for the News Enterprise in Hudson, Mass., where I was working. it was Bill Marlowe who suggested I do part time radio shows at WHET, located in Waltham, Mass. where Bill was broadcasting at the time. Backing up a bit, as a teenager I was a big fan of Bill Marlowe, like most teenagers. I remember going to his Record Hops, never dreaming that one day I'd be doing a radio show at the same station, with him as my teacher."

According to Frankie, Bill Marlowe was always very kind and helpful in teaching him how to handle the complicated radio equipment. Marlowe went all out to arrange for Frankie to visit a special studio to watch him record restaurant advertisements for his shows. When the other radio D.J's at WHET discovered Bill had asked Frankie to come into the recording studio, the remark was that Bill never permitted anyone ever to watch him record advertisements for his customers. Frankie had been most fortunate, because that was a first.

"I found Bill to be a very sincere gentle giant with friends including yours truly. I've seen both sides of this man. I saw the sadness and the tears rolling down his cheeks. Without doubt Bill Marlowe was a very compassionate human being who cared about people, places and things. He often asked me to join him for a few drinks at some of the best pubs and bars in Boston. When we would arrive at any bar, Bill was always welcomed with any drinks he desired, as well as I. I have to admit that in those days Bill and I enjoyed the booze, especially when it was gratis. I could never have afforded to drink in these plush clubs and bars.

"One thing I never forgot about this man who stuck by keeping the songs and big bands and singers from the 40's and 50's and 60's going. He refused to change his musical format. He endured ridicule from other disc jockeys who played as Bill named it, noise. He often would say over the airwaves; 'I play M-U-S-I-C not N-O-I-S-E!' While other disc jockey's were implicated in the radio payola scandal of the 1950's, he was considered one of the few broadcasters above suspicion. Bill always said; 'They knew no one was paying me to play Frank Sinatra, Sarah Vaughan, Erroll Garner, Dakota Staton and Tony Bennett.'"

Bill Marlowe Productions

Personalized Programming

May 10, 1996

Dear Friend Frank,

A bit late getting this off because of having to be confined to the hospital again. So much for being to hell and back.

Now, I hope all is well with you, in the event people neglect to place accolades on you for all you're doing, let me bestow kudos and commendations upon you for your untiring efforts and contributions for senior [Senior] citizens, many of them, among the forgotten. Bravo Frank.

My best to Terry Robinson for the portrait and my love, as always to you Frank. Stay healthy Frank and never take health for granted." I never forgot your courage and the strength, will, fortitude and determination it took for you to stop drinking – Bravo!!!

Much Love your friend
Bill M.

Frank, Please send my article Copies in the American Liberty News to the Boston Mass General Hospital.

I RECALL

Ron Della Chiesa
A Humble Giant of the Aiarwaves

Massachusetts Broadcasters Hall of Fame
At Masgasott Community College
Hall of Fame: 2013
Ron Della Chiesa

Ron landed his first radio job at WBOS, hired by Arnie "Woo Woo" Ginsberg, to host a series of ethnic radio shows. After a stint in the US Army, he joined classical music station WBCN. When WBCN changed to a rock-n-roll format, he moved to WGBH-FM, a relationship that continues to this day.

Quincy native Ron Della Chiesa developed an early love for radio when he appeared at the age of 10 on a children's show on Quincy's local radio station, WJDA. Fascinated by this experience, he created a radio station in his bedroom, consisting of a cardboard microphone and record turntable writing his own commercials and newscasts, he began broadcasting to an imaginary audience. He also developed a passion for opera and classical music listening to his father's collection of Caruso records and other legendary tenors

While a student at the Boston University School of Communication, he landed his first radio job at WBOS to host a series of radio shows, including the Italian Melody Hour, the Polish Variety Hour, Music of the Near East, the Boston Greek Hour and the Irish Hour.

Later, Ron joined classical music station WBCN, eventually becoming Program Director. When WBCN changed to a Rock-n-Roll format, he moved to WGBH-FM, hosting the popular Music America show more than 18 years, where he interviewed great artists from the world of Opera, Broadway, Film, American Popular Song and Jazz, including Luciano Pavarotti, Eileen Farrell, Robert Merrill, Tony Bennett, Dizzy Gillespie, Buddy Rich, Stan Getz, Dave McKenna, Wynton Marsalis, John Williams, Keith Lockhart, Sammy

Cahn, Carol Channing, Rosemary Clooney, Harry Connick, Jr., and Frank Sinatra, Jr., to mention a few. He continues to act as the Host for the Boston Symphony Orchestra and Boston Pops live broadcasts from Symphony Hall and Tanglewood.

In January, 1997, Ron and his executive producer, Paul Schlosberg, inaugurated the Strictly Sinatra and Music America shows on WPLM-FM, Plymouth, that still continues Sunday evenings. He also hosts a show featuring Golden Memories of Yesteryear at www.GMMY.com.

Ron is a Boston University Distinguished Alumnus. He is also a winner of the 2010 Ovation Award from Opera Boston, the annual Public Action for the Arts, Man of the Year Award in 2003 and the National Jazz Educators of MA award for his efforts to bring Jazz and American Music to audiences in New England. To celebrate his 50 years in radio, he recently wrote "Radio My Way" with co-author Erica Ferencik. The book includes celebrity profiles from Jazz, Opera and the American Song Book.

Heading into his 75th year, Ron feels fortunate to still be sharing his love for radio with his many fans and friends. As he says: "Stay Tuned, the Best is Yet to Come!"

Ron Della Chiesa meets Terry Robinson in person for the first time to interview Terry Robinson in the early 1990's. L-R: Ron, d his wife Joyce, Terry Robinson and me. Both Ron Della Chiesa and Terry Robinson wrote articles for the American Liberty News.

The Best in Music with Ron Della Chiesa

Radio Stations should jump on booking Ron Della Chiesa's "Music America" Show. Since 1960, when Ron Della Chiesa joined the happy WGBH-FM radio family. He has become one of New England's well-known radio and television personalities.

Ron Della Chiesa, is noted for filling the airwaves with the best in classical music from opera to the great masters of Symphonies at radio station WGBH-FM Boston. Ron is also noted for his musical adventure with his popular radio shows, "Music America", and "Strictly Sinatra" shows as well.

The "Music America," show, originated in September 1977 by Della Chiesa at WGBH-FM, from that point on, this great show went on to become one of New England's loved and talked about radio musical shows. However the "Music America" show is aired from another popular radio station WPLM-FM in Boston on Saturday nights from 7-to-12 midnight.

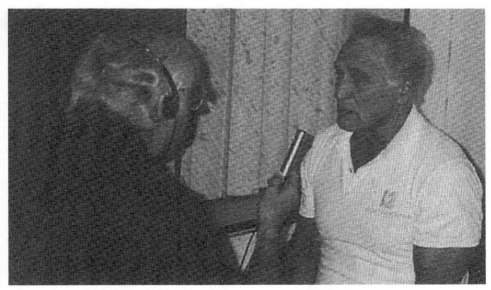

Terry Robinson

Presently, Ron's "Music America" show is being aired over WPLM-FM from 7-to-12 midnight on Saturdays. And I am proud to announce Ron's shows have been with GMMY RADIO for 11 years. His shows air every morning from 6 to 8:30 a.m.

Ron's "Music America" and "Strictly Sinatra" show had become a big hit at WGBH and now at WPLM. He continues to expand the Music America's format to include live performances and special features from the greatest musical talents of the big band era to their popular vocalists, such as Tony Bennett, Frank Sinatra, Al Martino, Jerry Vale and many more outstanding entertainers.

Ron Della Chiesa has also been the host and master of ceremonies for numerous events in and around the greater Boston area, including the Boston globe Jazz Festival, the Jazz Boat cruises, and concerts at Symphony Hall. On Sundays, he broadcasts a live classical show from Tanglewood. He's a busy radio host who keeps us all informed on the good "M-U-S-I-C, and not the N-O-I-S-E!"

Ron Della Chiesa A Humble Giant Of 'The Airwaves'

Ron Della Chiesa, is the only radio host I know of that hosts Classical Music, Opera, popular music of the great singers of the 50's, plus does a jazz show. In the evenings he is known to trade in his daily congenial wardrobe for a tux, to hosts the live Boston Symphony Orchestra, or do his live Tanglewood Show on Sunday's at Tanglewood, Massachusetts. Not only does he host Classical live concerts. Ron also hosts numerous Jazz Shows live, at various jazz concerts, all over New England to New York City.

Ron Della Chiesa, is one of the most humble human beings I have had the pleasure of meeting in my life time. He's down to earth, no fanfares, and mingles in with all types of people, be they from the streets or from the elite. He is loved by all. He has never forgotten where he came from.

In many wonderful phone conversations with my good buddy Ron Della Chiesa, it's always a pleasure and an honor to hear his views about the good music and his appearances, be them at night clubs or opera radio shows, the man stays musically busy. I have had the honor of being his friend for so many a year. "Big Ron," as I call him, is indeed a connoisseur of the great classical music, and opera, and popular music. Ron is a legendary icon, of good music, if you will, in keeping the good music alive. AH! As we would say in many Italian words; 'Squsito,' 'Elegante,' 'Numero Uno.' … And this is what Ron Della Chiesa is all about.

Our phone conversations were of the great music of the 40's, 50's, 60's in which Ron continues to play on his shows daily, and weekends. We talked about the great tenors, and about the great singers and the big bands. But most important of all, we talked about the good ole days of radio when most stations were playing the good stuff and as the late Bill Marlowe used to say "I play Good M-U-S-I-C and not N-O-I-S-E."

In Ron's own words he praised Al Martino as "One of the best Belcanto Voices in the world of popular show biz." Ron went on to say: "I play Al Martino's recordings in all my shows... He is a part of my format." In the past Ron even interviewed Al Martino on August 25, 2004. This same interview is often aired on Gmmy Radio in which Ron Della Chiesa's shows are played daily every morning from 6 a.m. up to 8:30 a.m. I cannot thank Ron Della Chiesa enough. He has been with Gmmy Radio for the past 11 years, and as I always say; Ron 'keeps the good music swinging and never takes a licking.'

Speaking to Ron over the phone brought back fond memories of my own radio days in the 70's over station WHET, now defunct, when I also had the honor to work with another giant of radio. None other than the late Bill Marlowe who took me under his wing to teach me the way of running the radio equipment for broadcasting over the airwaves,

Often times I had the pleasure to dine out with these two giants. Ron Della Chiesa, and Bill Marlowe, either at the ("European" restaurant) now gone, or the 'Roma' restaurant, located in the Italian section of Boston... "The North End." As always our discussions were of the great popular singers and the big bands.

Today Ron Della Chiesa, still has a website called: "Spirit Of Sinatra" which is linked-up in our Frank Sinatra web page on Golden Music Memories Of Yesteryear at this URL; www.gmmy.com '.' Every Saturday night Ron hosts a special Sinatra show titled: "Strictly Sinatra" which airs from 7:00 P.M.-to-Midnight over station WPLM-Easy 99.1 FM. Ron also hosts the popular "Music America" show at WPLM which airs on Sundays 7:00 P.M. -to- Midnight.

Ron praised the Gmmy web site, he said it was 'unbelievable'. He said the Crooners and tenors web pages were fantastic. I thank you Ron for your kind words. I have never known Ron Della Chiesa to talk down about any vocal artist, or musician, or anyone else for that matter. Ron Della Chiesa is a very compassionate human being who is well loved by numerous vocal artists, jazz musicians, and the great tenors of our day, and numerous friends. One of his good friends who often time will visit Ron at his home is singer Tony Bennett, who both have been close friends for more years than I can count. As a matter of fact, Tony Bennett's daughter lived with the Della Chiesa's while attending college in Boston.

In the past on my visits to Boston I always made sure to visit Ron at his home; he has got to be one of the world's best collectors of music memorabilia. On his walls hang numerous art work drawn or painted by his good friend Tony Bennett. He even has one of Al Martino's rare 78's. Visiting Ron's home is like taking a wonderful tour of a museum of the great singers, jazz musicians of the past, and present.

It is always an honor to be able to either call Ron Della Chiesa via phone or visit him when I go to Boston to visit my relatives and friends. And as our mutual late friend Bill Marlowe use to say; "Ronnie you're the living end."

Al Martino, Ron Itri, and Ron Della Chiesa

Attorney Ron Itri [Center] Was Very Instrumental In Putting The Package Of The Oct. 7, 1999 'Mario Lanza Day' Proclamation together with Argeo Cellucci Jr. as a special guest on Ron Della Chiesa's show.

I RECALL

GMMY Radio

It's GMMY Radio's 12th Birthday
Feb-20, 2016

We Have The Smack Others Lack:

WE FEATURE THESE SENSATIONAL SINGERS: Perry Como, Frank Sinatra, Al Martino, Vic Damone, Dean Martin, Tony Bennett, Arthur Prysock, Nat King Cole, Jerry Vale, Frankie Laine, Don Cornell, Frankie Finelli, Mario Lanza, Buddy Clark, Sammy Davis, Jr., Mel Torme, Nancy Wilson, Billie Holiday, Judy Garland, Jimmy Durante, Dinah Shore, Bobby Darin, Bing Crosby, Dinah Washington, Ella Fitzgerald, Patti Page, Peggy Lee, Natalie Cole, Jack Jones, Count Basie, Artie Shaw, Glenn Miller, Louis Armstrong and many more.

Chances are you won't hear all these great singers and big band sounds on a lot of other radio stations - stay tuned to GMMY radio for the best in pop and good classical music and more!!

TUNE IN TO OUR SUPERB GMMY RADIO HOSTS: Ron Della Chiesa, Steve Slezak, Harry & Lena Smith Show, Alan Brown, Frank Sinclair, And From Italy; Mr. Giuliano Fournier, Dick & Shirley Finnell Shows, Frank E. Dee, And The National Taxpayers Union With Pete Sepp.

A special mention goes to author of the century, and our honorary GMMY websites and radio president Dr. Richard Grudens - you can read more about the Song Stars and Music Men on his Website: http://www.richardgrudens.com.

Tune Into Gmmy - It's A Slice Of Heaven

Our radio hosts' can make your day a lot lighter and brighter.

There are so many negative things occurring in our world today - not a day passes without seeing something revolting in a newspaper or on 'smellervision' or 'stinkervision' [as I call TV]. Politicians overspending taxpayers' money, crimes being committed in our streets, murders, shootings, and rape, which is a disgrace, and now beheadings - something unheard of back in the day - surely alcoholism and drugs are a huge factor in the increase of such crimes - it seems these things grow worse on a daily basis. With all of the terrible news and garbage that bombards and smothers us, there is somewhat of an escape - that escape could be simple even if it's for a few hours or so - how? by sitting back in your favorite easy chair and turning on good nostalgic music that Gmmy Radio Hosts provide for your listening pleasure - from orchestras such as Mantovani, tJackie Gleason or 101 Strings, and your favorite singers.

Listening to good music has the power to take you on an escape from the present stress in society via wonderful memories, be they of love, romance or laughter. These favorite songs have the power to take you wherever you wish to go. Even our cats or our dogs love the soothing sounds of good music, and all I know is it works for them as well as for us humans.

For instance, just think of all the couples who have "their song." or the people that end up connecting because of similar tastes in the good stuff that I call good nostalgic music. Gmmy Radio sticks to the format of good music of the 30's, 40's and 50's and 60's because it can go deep within the soul and it is not only humans but also animals who enjoy good relaxing music. Trust me when I write, my two pets [two dogs] love being in the Gmmy Radio studio, it's like they are in a comfort zone of security. I repeat, for instance, different types of nostalgic music can provoke different reactions in animals and humans and is further proof that there is something about nostalgic music that can reach far deeper than we can understand. Good music for sure can be soothing and relaxing, and even help to keep folks healthy, and closer together, especially after you've had a long hard day. What better way is there to relax to the sounds of good music?

Throughout life, most folks will develop a taste for music. Some music types will stay forever and others will change throughout our lives. This often depends on what is going on in our lives at any given time and because we associate different songs with different events, times, ages and emotions, and relationships.

Immediately when We hear our favorite tunes we are transported in our minds eye back to whatever was going on at the time and we relive the same feelings. These may fade slightly over time but they remain.

I find that for myself, music can be such a huge reminder of the good old days that it helps to escape from the reality of the present. People who enjoy good music that lifts your mood and gives a joyful feeling

L-R: Paul Tanner, Jim Priddy, Frank D'Anolfo and Glenn Miller

use it deliberately to alter their mood. For those who want to, they can create an easy does it day or a romantic atmosphere with some mellow love songs from our great singers. All you have to do is tune into Gmmy Radio to hear your favorite songs and singers and it don't cost a cent to enjoy our musical format, and as the old saying goes "if music be the food of love and of life, play on and on," and at Gmmy Radio that is exactly what our radio hosts do.

You can tune into GMMY RADIO daily to hear the good music and singers of the great era of the 30's, 40's, 50's, and 60's. Visit our websites and vist the following URL's: Gmmy Radio Web Page: www.gmmy.com/GMMYRADIO.htm or our GMMY website: www.gmmy.com.

You'll be happy you stopped by.

Famous Band Leaders of the 1950's

BAND LEADERS IN THE 1950's

TOP ROW L-R: STAN KENTON, LAWRENCE WELK, LES BROWN, HARRY JAMES, RAY ANTHONY, FREDDY MARTIN, ORRIN TUCKER.
BOTTOM ROW L-R: SAM DONAHUE, WOODY HERMAN, LeROY ANTHONY, JERRY GRAY.

My Favorite Menu Of Music:
Make Mine Just Pure Nostalgic Music

Most of my life I've admired and loved the good music of the 30's, 40's and 50's, 60's. What I never understood was why some singers who sing, sang in full voice yet, were called crooners. I always thought a crooner was somewhat of a type of voice that would add a ... "Ba-Ba-Ba-Boo" sound, like Bing Crosby used to do (and no offene to Bing, as I was a big fan of his). To me that was what I thought crooning was.

I have and always will be hooked on good Music with beautiful lyrics that I could understand which were meaningful, loving, and had the power to bring back beautiful fond memories. It was through this type of music that led me to become a radio host. The beauty of being the host of my own radio show was that I was allowed to play the music I loved and adored for the same group of audiences, who also admired and loved these same great songs sung by the artists who made them popular. Songs that could make the goose bumps stand-up like little tin soldiers. And songs with clean cut lyrics!

I have spent a lifetime writing articles, and short stories on the great singers of those golden days, some who still perform to worldwide record breaking audiences. Although some have passed on, their voice and songs are kept alive on our Gmmy Radio. And thank God for all our radio hosts who work hard in keeping the good music flowing over our radio airwaves.

My pay back to good MUSIC, and the great singers and a dream I had, was to create one of the best entertainment web sites that are geared to promoting these fantastic singers and their songs along with the great big bands. When I chose the title name I created "GOLDEN MUSIC MEMORIES OF YESTERYEAR" for short GMMY RADIO, for the web site. I was told "It won't work." or "The name is too long," or "Who is going to care to listen to those singers." Well, I'll tell you who cares, the listening audience who tune into our Gmmy Radio, who enjoy the good music of the big bands and the singers of those golden years of the 30's on up into the 60's. That's who cares!

As my good colleague friend the late Bill Marlowe once told me "If you don't want to help me, then get the heck out of my way and let me do what I have to do." A pure super suggestion and a point well made by my good friend Bill Marlowe, who has always lived by this golden rule of thumb. And if Bill Marlowe was alive today he'd be right on Gmmy Radio playing the great big band sounds and the great singers.

We at Gmmy Radio promote singers and big bands not for the sake of "what's in it for us." It's a labor of love! We at Gmmy Radio do not have our hand out looking for a buck. Our belief is to carry the musical message of the great singers and their songs to those who will enjoy the good music. And we do this for fun and for free. And that's the name of our tune. And so the simplicity of creating the "Golden Music Memories of Yesteryear" web site and Gmmy Radio is not about an ego thing or making a buck. No! It's about keeping the good Music, and the artists of a wonderful era flowing daily over our websites and airwaves. And I do believe in time these same songs sung by these great artists who sang them will never be for-

gotten. GMMY is here to educate an upcoming generation about the good music and stars who perform these great songs. Trust me when I write here that we have spent countless hours promoting all the singers on our web sites and on Gmmy Radio.

Rosemary Clooney, Frank Sinatra, Dean Martin (Top) Kathryn and Bing Crosby Bottom Right

By the way and this has nothing to do with radio, but if you have not experienced a trip across the USA with Amtrak, in a private room, you're sure missing out on a royal treat of seeing the countryside scenery and the beautiful Rockies. Just another thought on enjoying life and wholesome pleasure.

Alan Brown From England
Salutes Gmmy Radio
By Alan Brown

Being the presenter of The Vocal Touch programs over GMMY RADIO I would like to say a few words about the other presenters here on GMMY RADIO.

The presenters that put on programs containing the sounds of good music are as follows: Harry and Lena Smith, Frank Sinclair, Ron Della Chiesa, Dick and Shirley Finnell, Steve Slezak, and the boss man himself Frankie Dee all of whom present music from the 30s 40s 50s and into the 60s by artists you won't hear on other stations. I know you can hear Vic Damone, Frank Sinatra, Perry Como, and Tony Bennett on most stations, but where will you hear artists like Curt Massey, Johnnie Johnston, Dennis Day, John Gary, Billy Eckstine, Ed Ames, among others.

GMMY RADIO is truly a station where you will hear all the great singers, bands, jazz and female singers along with the best selection of opera and the classics from both sides of the pond.

Harry and Lena Smith who present their programs from London, play all of the English artists, their collection of material is unbelievable, and the thing is you never hear the artists they play being played on British radio, it's then you realize what a gem GMMY RADIO is.

All the presenters have their programs aired daily and one of them is Frank Sinclair. Now this gentleman's (The Sentimental Gentleman of the Airwaves) program, Anything Goes, is crammed full of goodies and wonderful air checks from old time American comedy programs, so don't miss it.

Ron Della Chiesa will more than keep the Sinatra fans happy with his Strictly Sinatra programs and another daily broadcast, Music America, which contain a great selection of music - the type of which you will only hear every day on GMMY RADIO. When it comes to the pop music of the 40s and the 50s Dick and Shirley Finnell really come up with the winners and if they don't play it, it wasn't recorded.

Whilst GMMY RADIO caters better than any other radio station to people who's interests are the best of popular music of the decades of the 30s 40s and 50s, they also come up with the goods when you want to hear classical music and opera - you won't find a more knowledgible man than Mr. Steve Slezak he is a gold mine of information and well worth a listen, you better believe it.

Finally the boss man himself - the man that makes it all happen - Mr. Frankie Dee - what can I say about him, other than *stay tuned* because you never know what he'll come up with.

So all in all GMMY RADIO, which is aired worldwide via the internet is the place to be.

HAPPY LISTENING, Alan Brown!

Dedicated to Frankie Dee by Alan Brown from England

I'm Alan Brown from England and I would like to write a few words about a man by the name of Frankie Dee, a man of few words but who gets on and gets things done.

I got to know Frankie Dee through radio, exactly how, I honestly don't recall.

It all started by the fact that I had always wanted to do a radio program of good listening music but nobody wanted to know Alan Brown. Who's he? He certainly was unknown, but by sheer chance Frankie Dee came to my attention via the internet. I contacted him by sending him a pilot program. He immediately accepted me and from then on became one of my closest friends and we remain in close contact via our computers. He in America and I in merry old England.

Frankie started his radio station GMMY RADIO against all odds being told it wouldn't catch on but eleven years later his idea has a big following and a group of fine presenters who do programs for the station. Frankie has stuck by his idea and as I have said before he got the job done, very successfully.

But forgetting the radio thing, he does a lot of good in his local community which he never talks about, also he does a lot of work for a local church in helping recovering alcoholics.

A few years back I had the privilege of meeting Frankie Dee and having met him I consider it was a privilege. It is a pity that there are not more of the likes of Frankie Dee. For if there were the world would be a better place to live in.

The GMMY RADIO project has a policy of playing good listening music and being in charge of GMMY RADIO, Frankie Dee makes sure that the music played is the type that won't offend anyone. No smut, no offensive language. And for that alone you have to admire the man in today's world.

Finally I would like to say that I hope Frankie Dee has many more years at the helm of GMMY RADIO and that I may be part of it. He has done a lot for me. I also know he has done a lot for many others. Frankie, long may I be your friend and I thank you for being my friend.

Sincerely, Alan Brown

Alan Brown

Dick & Shirley Finnell
An Honored Gmmy Family Member

Two Wonderful Al Martino Fans Make It All Happen

It was a rare treat having Pennsylvanians's Dick & Shirley Finnell as our first Gmmy Radio hosts. They literally helped me kick off our musical format of the great songs performed by the legendary crooners backed by the big band sounds of Benny Goodman to Glenn Miller and beyond. Dick and Shirley were also instrumental in getting Gmmy Radio on the airwaves. It is pure magic having such great radio hosts, now permanent members who have become an important member of the Gmmy Radio family airwaves since the opening on February 20, 2004.

Dick & Shirley were truly archive specialists in the field of collecting rare recordings, CD's, and tapes of the great singers and big bands of the 30's, 40's, 50's up to the 60's and the good music that we all remember. They too were in the same music zone of Harry & Lena Smith from England, who share with us all, a lovable caring feeling that makes you feel you've known them a life time.

Dick & Shirley Finnell, were quick to support the Gmmy web sites by sharing their posting on the Al Martino message forum. Thus from there came the start of a family of wonderful friends, that became like one big happy family.

I was deeply honored to have chosen them in tribute also as "Our GMMY FAMILY," for all they have done in being so supportive and giving of themselves to all who joined in on the Al Martino web site and on Gmmy Radio as a big part of our family team. Both Dick & Shirley Finnell have also been very generous in donating numerous tapes of various singers and the big bands to my Frank E. Dee Shows which aired over Crusade Radio before Gmmy Radio started. Without Dick & Shirley, the Frank E., Dee Show would not have been as successful as it became. We thank Harry & Lena, who are close friends to Dick & Shirley Finnell.

To Dick & Shirley Finnell: I adored and love you both for being there for me through hard times and the good times when I was starting up the GMMY RADIO Shows. I remember a lot of people telling me "It can't be done". To those non-believers I say it was done!! Thanks be to you Dick & Shirley Finnell, Gmmy Radio features a good family of hosts, who produce their great musical formats of the 'GOOD STUFF' as I called it. God Bless you both.

Ballads For Bathing Beauties

Dick Finnell created this CD, a total surprise to me, and sent it to me with a beautiful listing of Al Martino's song's. Dick Finnell and his wife Shirley were the first Gmmy Radio Hosts on Gmmy Radio. The little doggie in the pool with me was Gina my first Golden Retriever. Her name was taken from my parent's town in Italy. Gina loved swimming with anyone who went into the pool. He always kicks off his show with one of Al Martino's songs. If I'm not mistaken I think Dick Finnell had every recording that Al Martino recorded. I'll never forget you Dick for all you did for Gmmy Radio and Gmmy Websites. I know you're upstairs with the angels playing Al Martino's songs. We all loved you, and miss you.

What a surprise it was when Dick & Shirley created this special Al Martino CD titled Al Martino Sings Ballads for Bathing Beauties with the photo of yours truly with my first Golden Retriever Gina in a pool.

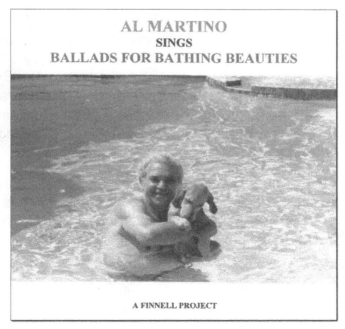

AL MARTINO
SINGS
BALLADS FOR BATHING BEAUTIES

A FINNELL PROJECT

The Good Music From England
On GMMY Radio
Thanks To Our Radio Hosts
Harry & Lena Smith
and Alan Brown From England

Gmmy Radio is proud and honored to air some of the best vocalists and big band sounds from England every morning and even during the day. Thanks to Harry and Lena Smith and Alan Brown who took yours truly under their wings to educate me about the great sounds of the English bands and pop singers of which I was not aware.

How could I have been so darn naive to think America was the only country in the world to have great jazz bands, and super popular singers, not to mention great opera singers? How wrong was I. But how grateful I am that three of the nicest people came into my life back in the year of 2004 and introduced me to the legends of England. They went all out to supply some of the best pop singers and big bands of England, now featured every day on Gmmy Radio.

Some of the great vocal legends of the UK are Matt Monro, Dickie Valentine, Issy Bonn, Al Bowlly, Denny Dennis, Jimmy Young, Dick James, Vince Hill, Steve Conway, Sir Harry Secombe, David Hughes, and the list goes on and on. Some of the Big Bands like the Harry Roy Band, Carroll Gibbons and his Orchestra, Ted, Heath, Joe Loss, and of course Ray Noble, Freddy Gardner, and so many more. What a great run of music these legends swing out on Gmmy Radio.

I honestly doubt if there are many radio stations in the U.S.A. who spotlight some of the wonderful singers and big bands from England who are featured daily on American radio. And if not, what a shame. However, it's their loss - Gmmy Radio's gain.

Julian-The Radio Man

My name is Giuliano (Julian) Fournier and I always wanted to be a radioman. I started collecting records when I was very young. I was working for SETAF, US Forces as a civilian in Italy, in the cities of Verona and Vicenza. I became friends with my boss Sgt. Raymond Bowles, he was a Frank Sinatra fan. At the time, my dream was to get into the PX, and see LPs that were available. These records were coming into the PX much earlier than in the Italian record stores.

I remember the first 78 rpm record I bought. It was "From Here to Eternity" by Frank Sinatra. That was the year 1955. As the years went by, my collection significantly increased. I became so fanatic that I wanted to express my musical taste to other people. Therefore, I tried to get a job at a radio station. A steady job. In 1973, I went to Radio della Svizzera Italiana (Italian Swiss Radio) and I offered my expertise. They told me: "Let's see what you can do." In the meantime I had the chance to meet several great

singers and musicians such as pianist Jose Iturbi, bandleader Count Basie, Duke Ellington, Stan Kenton (whom I considerd my Godfather), famed vocalists Sarah Vaughan, Ella Fitzgerald, and later on Frank Sinatra, Johnnie Ray, Dean Martin, Frankie Laine, Al Martino, Pat Boone, and Tony Bennett. Stan Kenton was performing in Milano, Italy, so I went to see him and told him "Stan, I have the chance to work for Swiss Radio, would you give me an interview?" He replied: "I can do more than that, I will also let you record part of the show." I did a radio program and I got the job! I worked at Radio della Svizzera Italiana as a broadcaster for 30 years.

More recently, I had the chance to became friends with the son of another idol, the great Mario Lanza, his son Damon Lanza, and the historian Bob Dolfi. They introduced me to GMMY RADIO and Frank Dee, I am so happy now to be part of the Gmmy Radio family.

Giuliano's show airs on Gmmy Radio on Saturdays at 12 noon pacific standard time.

Celebrates it's 12th Year Broadcasting Worldwide on Feb. 20, 2016

Thanks go all out to our Gmmy Radio Hosts; Ron Della Chiesa, Steve Slezak, Alan Brown, Harry Smith, Frank Sinclair, Dick & Shirley Finnell Shows, Juliano Fornier, Frank E. Dee

Gmmy Radio Continues
Spreading The Gospel Message of Nostalgic Music

Its A Slice Of Heaven Broadcasting Worldwide
FEATURING THE NOSTALGIC SONGS AND SINGERS
OF THE 30'S, 40'S, 50'S, AND 60's

**Gmmy Radio Is Also On WI-FI RADIO
To Tune In Go to this link:
https://forum.reciva.com/**

WiFi Internet Radio lets you listen to Internet radio stations without a computer and has the highest quality audio among WiFi radios.

**Also Visit Our Gmmy Radio Web Page At:
www.gmmy.com/GMMYRADIO.htm
Or Our GMMY WEBSITE: www.gmmy.com**

**You Now Can Use Windows Media Player Button
To Tune Into Gmmy Radio, Or The Winamp Button**

**Go to The following URL's Below
http://azulweb.streamguys.com/gmmy.asx
For Winamp Use:
http://war.str3am.com:7350/listen.pls**

Steve Slezak

Steve was one of our first Classical GMMY Radio Hosts.

Tune in daily to Steve Slezak's 'Collector's Vault Show' from Monday thru Fridays 10:00 A.M. to 11:00 A.M.

Afternoons from 4:00 P.M. To 5:00 P.M. Sunday's from 9:00 A.M. To 10:00 A.M. And Sunday afternoons from 3:00 to 4:00 P.M.

Steve Slezak is one of the best classical opera radio hosts of the airwaves and it is an honor to have Steve on Gmmy Radio.

Steve began his broadcast career with WSUI/KSUI-FM, Iowa City, Iowa, in October of 1966. From 1968 through 1972, he was with the Armed Forces Radio and Television service, in the Air Force, stationed numerous places in this country, and at Trabzon and Diyarbakir, Turkey, y in Vietnam, and lastly, Upon, Thailand, where he met his wife, Playung.

For 27 years, he ran "The Collector's Vault", an international tape recording service, specializing in rare opera and concert performances, rare discs, etc. He maintains this name for the series running on Gmmy Radio & Crusade Radio. Steve was an announcer/producer/head of Traffic and Operations at WSUI/KSUI-FM in Iowa

By-the-way, the television anchors, Carol Simpson, John Cochran and Tom Brokaw, and the late actor, Greg Morris, got their starts at WSUI.

To Purchase Steve's Classical Cassettes and Recordings -- E-Mail Steve Slezak: spcv1@netzero.ne, or visit The Collector's Vault on Gmmy Radio Website.

A Special GMMY Radio Bulletin

Meet Lena & Harry Smith from England:

You are perhaps wondering who are Harry & Lena Smith. Well, they are an outstanding and most charming couple from merry old England who have been instrumental in spreading friendship, love and kindness to GMMY Radio listeners.

Both Lena & Harry have consistently reached out to all of our Gmmy Radio audiences keeping alive, the good music of the 40's, 50's and 60's since we started Gmmy Radio.

It is indeed a pleasure to pay tribute to these two wonderful people who have taken precious time to reach out and provide the best and rare music via radio from a variety of singers and the big bands who backed them.

By their efforts, they have made GMMY Radio a great place for our fans to enjoy superb music. I thank Lena & Harry Smith for all they have done in bringing good people and good music together within our happy GMMY Radio family featuring rare recordings every morning from 8:30 a.m. to 9:30 a.m. six days a week.

Lena and Harry Smith

Our Great Seniors Love Good Music

I have been asked many a time "How old are you.?" I never hide my age - I am 80 years old, born on the 14th day of June 1935, also known as is 'Flag Day.' I have the most wonderful senior friends who have devoted a lifetime helping other human beings. They are givers and not takers. The almighty buck is not their God, and they make it known to the takers and users and the greedy. Their goal is simple - just helping one another, while they enjoy good books, good reading, and watching the old films of the 40's up into the 60's when good movies were clean and not filled with cursing and sexual scenes. They love good musical films, a la Fred and Ginger, and so do I. I always adore the clean-cut humor, and I quote; "Don't worry about avoiding temptation — as you grow older, it starts avoiding you." Or as they would frequently say: "Age is just a number. Mine is unlisted."

I have learned a lot from the elderly and I'm still learning. who was told that the Key of Life is to be a better spiritual person each day, and at my age I'm still learning from those gentle giants. My good friends strive to become even better than they were yesterday. Not a day goes by when one of us hook up to enjoy a refreshing cup of coffee and talk about the good music and the bands we used to dance to in our youth.

After spending some enriching time with my senior friends, and hearing all about the good music of our era, I find myself thinking of the past, like most of us do, and I often remember those wonderful lyrics of songs and the matchless sound of big band music and the great singers who sang those beautiful lyrics we all understood. These songs had the power to bring those of us from the 1940's on up into the 1950's and 1960's right down memory lane. You could be driving your car and pull up to a traffic light and your ears would be greeted by the music of perhaps Harry James, in the vehicle next to you. I would toot my horn gently to greet a gentleman and give a thumbs up for playing some good swinging music, which, to me, was a slice of heaven. That's a miracle today, because often, when you're driving your car and you approach a red light, you're greeted with loud noise and rotten lyrics that you can't even understand.

Most seniors I know don't like hearing the obnoxiously loud and mostly annoying booming songs because they were raised on the good music of the big band era.

Interestingly enough, there are laws that govern how loud you can play your car stereo in California, and I quote: "California's Vehicle Code 27007 makes it illegal to play music in a vehicle that can be heard fifty feet away or more. It is a infraction, imposing a fine that can be several hundred dollars, including all the penalties and fees that are added onto the base fine."

Good move, California!

Crank Up The Sound For Senior's

I have fun with seniors - it's enjoyable. I'm not one to be a braggart, and I stay away from people who swear, but I like to joke with my elder friends who are aware of that special letter which 'I' joke about...the letter 'I.' I avoid certain individuals who constantly say 'I' 'I' 'I'. Then to be humorous 'I' ask these individuals' how do you spell 'I?' On the serious side I do have a lot of clean fun with people that I enjoy being with, and I like to bring a chuckle to the seniors and younger set with clean-cut humor.

While I'm visiting some of my friends at the senior centers, they often tell me they can't watch television due to their inability to hear the newer actors and actresses of this generation who speak their lines in a whisper, and when they do seam to speak up louder it's so you can hear their foul language more so than their regular lines - what a disgrace.

Or are these modern actors and actresses not projecting their voices enough ? I hear more and more from people who watch these so called new actors and actresses say to me "what the heck did he or she say?" It seems like everyone I talk to tells me they have to pump up the volume on their TV to try and figure what these actors are saying. They seem to talk in a whisper. In contrast, if you were to listen to the legendary actors of the 40's and 50's speaking, like James Earle Jones, you clearly understand every single word this man says -- without having to pump up the sound.

A question to our readers who may recall the great films of the 1940's and 50's? Did you ever have to pump up the television sound or strain to hear such greats as Edward G. Robinson, Chuck Heston, Betty Davis, Glenn Ford, Humphrey Bogart, 'Duke' John Wayne, Jimmy Stewart, Richard Widmark, Burt Lancaster, Gary Cooper, Kirk Douglas? Heck no!! Even new radio hosts seem to follow the same suit. What is it with this new style of whispering lines? You may also remember the big voices of such giant announcers as Marvin of the Arthur Godfrey show, and Frank Gallop of Perry Como's Show. At least you knew what they were saying. They spoke clearly and projected their voices.

Isn't it amazing that these 'Rock and Rap' singers, can blast you out of your shoes!! Yet when they speak in films or on stage it's a mere whisper! Yuk!!! The California police have been issuing a fine to every vehicle that blasts their audio CD's or radio when they approach a traffic signal. And so to my senior friends, good morning world, as William B. Williams used to say - with his golden voice on New York's WNEW radio for many years.

I'm on your side!

Author Richard Grudens with William B. Williams

Those Good Old Days Of The Fabulous 1950's
...And Kilroy Was Here Too

Kilroy was being posted every where we went.

The great 1940's and 1950's as I remember, were easier and more wonderful - when foul language was rarely used and most movies were clean-cut, and for those of us who lived in this period you will remember the great big bands and their wonderful vocalists who sang songs with meaningful lyrics that were easily understood. Remember those wonderful parades when men wore soft hats and removed them when the American Flag passed on by. Prayer was allowed in schools and in most public places, and drugs were not the way of life as it became in later years of the 80's and 90's on into the 2000's.

Kilroy Was Here!

These wonderful words "In God We Trust" were not just words printed and stamped on our currency, but meant so much to all of us. In those years, comedians and their comedy of the early television shows never allowed comedians to use the filthy jokes or foul language that is being used in today's stand-up comedy shows! My website, Golden Music Memories Of Yesteryear was built with the purpose in mind to continue to endorse those golden years of fine crooners, the great big bands, the articles, and photos and the numerous Message Boards of the great entertainers from an era that shall never be forgotten.

As long as GOLDEN MUSIC MEMORIES OF YESTER-YEAR's website is on the world wide internet, we shall continue to endorse the great talents of the those special years. We welcome you to partake of those great years once again for your musical enjoyment. We also endorse author Richard Grudens' sensational books covering the lives of all those superb entertainers.

An Article Appearing in The Community Advocate from Hudson MA.

Your Hometown News Source Since 1974. **CommunityAdvocate**

Hudson – In 1953, Dean Martin sang about the moon hitting "your eye like a big pizza pie." Through Frank DeSimone, better known as Frank E. Dee to his listeners, music fans can still get what he calls "a little slice of heaven."

Since February of 2004, DeSimone has broadcast GMMY radio from his home in Costa Mesa, Cal. GMMY stands for "Golden Music Memories of Yesteryear" and is a worldwide Internet radio station in which he streams the music of the 30s, 40s, 50s and 60s, featuring big band leaders and crooners like Martin, Al Martino, Frank Sinatra, Glenn Miller, Doris Day and Jerry Vale.

DeSimone, a former Hudson resident for 16 years, recently contributed a chapter to author Richard Grudens" book "Perfect Harmony: Singing Groups of the 20th Century," highlighting the career of the Ames Brothers. Combining his love of music and writing, the chapter marked the fourth time he has written with Grudens. He contributed to Grudens" other books, "Mr. Rhythm: A Tribute to Frankie Laine," "Star Dust: The Bible of the Big Bands" and "Sinatra Singing."

DeSimone said Grudens contacted him through his GMMY radio site, www.gmmy.com, about writing for the book, which is about the music of the Andrews Sisters, Beach Boys, Weavers and Supremes.

When Grudens writes about musicians, the focus is their music and not their personal lives. DeSimone added, "I believe that's the way to go."

Grudens, who lives in St. James, N.Y. added, "My books reflect [DeSimone's] quest to keep the quality music of the 30s, 40s and beyond, and he does just that through his wonderful Internet radio show."

"The music was mostly wonderful, hummable and can fill you with joy," Grudens said.

Like Grudens, DeSimone has written about music and radio personalities for years. He said, "I like writing about people's lives."

DeSimone praised Grudens" work in chronicling the music of the big band era and classic crooners. He noted, "It's a beautiful thing. It's educational."

DeSimone lived in Hudson from 1960 to 1977, a time during which he was one of the advertising managers and a part-time columnist for the "Hudson News-Enterprise," a newspaper owned and published by Earle W. Tuttle.

He called Hudson a great place to live, adding, "I loved Hudson." He said Tuttle taught him about the newspaper business and meeting deadline. "He was the one who taught me how to type," DeSimone said. DeSimone interviewed "a lot of the stars," including singers like Don Cornell, a favorite of his. He met his idol while covering an event at the Bronx Lounge in Marlborough. He was trying to take photographs, but the area around the stage was crowded. Cornell stopped in the middle of his song and told everyone to "let that kid through." At first, DeSimone had no idea he was talking about him. Cornell let him come on stage and said, "Take all the pictures you want."

DeSimone, who was saddened by Cornell's death in 2004, added, "That was one I never forgot."

On the GMMY website, he recalled, "It was a Friday night, and there were lines waiting to hear Don display the same magical voice delivery and charm that made him famous. His voice was superb. He sang with great ease, poise and held his audience's attention."

DeSimone's job with the Hudson News-Enterprise segued into radio work. In the late 70s, he collaborated with Boston DJ and radio great Bill Marlowe of the now-defunct 1330 WHET-AM station. With Tuttle's support, he hosted the Frank E. Dee Show from 1976 to 1978. "That's a hell of a boss," DeSimone added.

Following Marlowe's passing in 1996, he wrote on the GMMY website: "Bill Marlowe became my radio mentor, my teacher."

Today, DeSimone is still in the radio business. The GMMY station boasts nine DJs and personalities from the United States, England and Italy, who are like family. He noted GMMY's accessibility: "Anybody who's got a computer can listen to GMMY radio." Although his goal is to "create the entertainment of my era," DeSimone loves what he's doing and has fun. He added, laughing, "You can's beat that."

DeSimone attributes a higher source for the many interesting directions his life has taken: "I think God takes you on different roads." Grudens said of DeSimone, "Frank has an uncanny sense of belief in everything he does. He is a generous, caring person who simply loves the music."

As always, it is about the music. Whether DeSimone is playing it or writing about it, the music of his generation remains close to his heart.

Golden Music Memories Of Yesteryear Website Receives 100 Awards

---

Below is a small sampling of the awards we have received by numerous companies and people.

The A1 Web Works Design Award
Congratulations ... Frank E. Dee

Your Web site has been selected to win a Web Works Site Award. My awards can not be downloaded from my pages they are e-mailed to you as an Attachment.

I have chosen your site, to be a "Kewl" site.

What is the purpose of this award? It is to signify that your site has been judged to contain quality content, design and/or HTML expertise.

What is my reason for giving awards? To give credit where credit is due. I know and you probably know that it takes a lot of time and effort to create a quality site. For this reason, I feel everyone who has achieved his or her goal of maintaining an overall "Kewl" site deserves at the least, a badge of honour. The badge of honour I have to offer is the Web Works Site Award. If you find that it has no meaning, it is just a graphic that someone created, then by all means, don't put it on your site. For those who appreciate the award, I am honoured to present it to you. This award is not given to everyone who nominates his or her home page or site. By my discretion, I pick only the sites I find to fit the minimum requirements and in some way or another soar beyond them.

Why do I have the authority to judge which sites are good and which sites are bad? I don't. I don't judge which sites are good or bad, I give the award to sites that in MY opinion are high quality. I judge the sites according to my own standards. I feel my standards are high, and I feel that it should be a proud thing to display the Web Works Site Award on your site.

Again, Congratulations!

Peter Williams, A1 Web Works Designs

The Bronze Gmmy Award

Congratulations! Your site has won the Bronze Wave Of The Web Award. Thanks for sharing your site with me. GMMY has a great design and is very informative. It is easy to tell you have put a lot of time and research into your web pages. Again congrats on your award. Your award is attached, and your site has been listed on my winners page.

Best of Luck,

Chad

The Golden Jewel Award

Dear Frank E. Dee,

Your website has given much pleasure to my Evaluation Panel Members during the evaluation process and we were impressed with the standard of quality you provided for viewing. We are fully aware that much time and effort goes into the creation of websites and we hope that you view this Award as a reflection of your achievement. We thank you for inviting us to visit with you and for your assisting through your website to make the World Wide Web a more pleasant area. Again, CONGRATULATIONS and thank you for the pleasure your website has given to my Evaluation Panel Members doing their visit to your site. They were pleased, keep up the work.

Regards, Jerry D.

The Silver Surfer Bronze 2000 Award

Greetings Frank,

We are proud to have the SilverSurfer on such a page as yours...It not only reflects your taste...But also ours..We thank you... Again...We are honored to have this award on your page...Congrats on a *BRONZE*...

You are one of the best.

Dear Frank E. Dee

In cooperation with my friend - professional Web-designer Kenn Sander have I evaluated your web-site. Congratulations I'm very pleased to present you with this "Award of Bronze". For your great site.

From The Roxy Website

Hello Frank,

I had a wonderful time visiting your website, truly! And am extremely happy to be able to give you an award! You have done a great job with your site, it's such a pleasure to visit :-) You've done so many "little things" that shows you really care about the music, and that says a lot!

I've added the link to your site already, on my page "Links To You". I'm so glad you invited me to visit your site, too! Keep up the great work :-) Roxy

---

"Superior Site Award": I have just had the opportunity to tour your site and was very impressed with the effort. Please accept the attached award, not an easy one to win, with my sincere congratulations.

"Congratulations! Your web-site has been reviewed and chosen to bear the 2000-2001 Golden Web Award".

From The "Award For Excellent Quality"... "Your homepage is really excellent!"

You have won the "2000 Humming Good Page" Award in recognition of all your hard work in creating your page. This award has been redesigned for the new millennium and I am sure you will be proud to display it on your page! I will add your Page and URL to the exclusive "Humming Good Page" award winners list at the next update.

I RECALL

Personal Reflections
Interviews and Stories of
The People Who Made
An Impression

Thank you Al Jolson

I was a mere 14 year old, shining shoes part time on week-ends at a shoe repair shop, and like most teens of that era, I want-ed to sing like Al Jolson, who appeared on radio shows like the Kraft Music Hall. It seemed everyone tried to imitate his singing style, including me when the 1947 movie *The Jolson Story* was featured in theaters in my home city of Somerville,. Mass. I remem-ber there were lines of people trying to purchase tickets to see one of the greatest entertainers of our time. I can boast that I saw this film over a dozen times, if not more, and when the second Jolson film came out *Jolson Sings Again* you can be sure I went to see this one a dozen times or more. I think every teen I chummed with felt the same way about seeing Larry Parks (he acted and Jolson sang) emulating one of the greatest singers of our time. Around our neighborhood many teens tried to sound like Al Jolson. I honestly believe there was not another singer that garnered so much atten-tion. There were record breaking lines of people seven days and nights waiting to get into the theaters, and for those of you reading this article who saw both Al Jolson films I'm sure you will remember them. These two films were terrific musical biography's that brought him back into the limelight and to great popularity, and I believe his comeback brought newer and younger fans to his fan base.

It was Al Jolson's singing that introduced yours truly to min-strel shows, and they were popular in the Vocational school I at-tended in my home city of Somerville, Mass. and in schools and theaters everywhere. Folks in our neighborhood whether African Americans, Irish or Italian or whatever race you were, all got along as though we were a big family, and everyone helped one anoth-er into blackening up their face. I remember one Halloween night burning a cork top from a bottle and spreading the burnt black cork all over my face to imitate Al Jolson. When my father saw this, he asked my mother to identify me.

Although Al Jolson had an immensely popular second career singing in both films, I became a big fan with my teenage friends, had it not been for those two films, we teens of the 50's would not have known who was Al Jolson. Sixty years later there is still an interest in listening to Al Jolson, America's Greatest Entertainer.

Thanks to Al Jolson for the wonderful popular songs he sang so well. However I became a big fan of Al Jolson, and his songs are featured daily on our GMMY RADIO.

Beverly Manning Owens on Bob Manning

Beverly Manning Owens, the daughter of the popular singer Bob Manning, hosted our Bob Manning's web site on the Gmmy Crooner Website. Beverly was always a wonderful Lady who helped make our crooner section a winner. She was a marvelous host and shared with all the Bob Manning fans on the Bob Manning Forum. We all will miss you Beverly.

Enclosed is a sad notice by Beverly Manning Owens by her husband Wayne P. Owens Sr. "I'm Beverly Manning Owens's husband, I am sorry to inform you that Beverly passed away on Saturday July 6, 2013. She was surrounded by her family, deeply-deeply loved by all her family and missed so very much each hour of each day."

The Bob Manning Gmmy web site and message forum will continue on in honor to Beverly Manning Owens and all the fans.

My Bob Manning Story

A True Story Written By
Dick Finnell, Our Gmmy Radio Host

In 1953 when I turned sixteen I had written a song and had 'Lenny Martin' arrange it and print it to sheet music. At sixteen I must have thought I was Irving Berlin. I gave copies to Tony Bennett and Al Alberts. (Al is probably still mad at me for waking him up at 10:00 in the morning). Bob Manning was appearing at Eddie Ashner's, a Supper Club outside of Pittsburgh. I didn't have a driver's license or car at that time. Nick Barbatti drove me to see Bob after his first show.

Unbelievably, Bob spent more time with me than some of my friends. Bob was 6'2" and towered over me. He treated me like a son. He actually put his arm around me and we walked to the piano. Bob's accompanist played, "I WAS A FOOL" for him. He liked it.

As luck and life goes, within a month, Nat "King" Cole released "A FOOL WAS I." I will never forget Bob's kindness and encouragement. I was a Bob Manning fan before I met him. His music is top shelf. I know it is one way, but on my side, he is still a friend.

Thank you Frank E. Dee, for providing the Gmmy Crooners site and for the opportunity to tell my story. Dick Finnell

In 1953 a young 16 year old boy from PITTS BURGH PA., was bitten by the talents of writing songs. At that era of time the young lad had wrote a song titled: "I WAS A FOOL." He had given copies of the song to pop singer Tony Bennett, and a copy to Al Alberts, who was the lead singer of the popular "FOUR ACES." However the lad didn't stop there. He took the liberty to walk the song into the hands of one of his favorite popular singers BOB MANNING, who took the time from his own busy schedule to spend with this young lad from Pittsburgh, PA.

Through my own personal experiences. I have found that

there are two breeds of entertainers:

A Special thank you to Dick Finnell one of the kindest caring human being I have had the honor of him being a great Gmmy Radio Host

1. There are those who are egotistical, controlling, with a prima donna attitude who have forgotten where they came from who wouldn't give you the right time of day. And for them, I don't even bother writing about on the Gmmy forums especially those who curse.

2. Then there are those fabulous entertainers, who never forgot where they came from, who are grateful for being where they are today, and these type of entertainers are well aware that it's the so called small wheels that make the big wheels turn - meaning the fans - who can make and break an entertainer. They are the ones who buy their records.

The History Of The Bust to Honor Harold W. Richards

How This Bust Became A Reality Thanks be to: Frank Ivanovich - By Frank E. Dee

"What You See Is What You Get"

This story is about a tribute idea I had to honor Harold W. Richards, founder of the Mesa Halfway House (a place where men can find help and support to overcome addition to alcohol). I personally sought to honor this man, and in my opinion it was a good thing to do. However before Mr. Richards had passed away, the idea I had was to have a plaque made-up in honor of his work, contribution and devotion in creating a non-profit recovery home for men who suffered under alcohol abuse. I wanted to honor him while he was still alive.

One day, while sitting in his back yard, as we often did, I told Mr. Richards that he deserves some kind of recognition in the form of a plaque dedicated in his honor for all his efforts in making the halfway house what it had become. However, Harold was never one to seek glory or accolades for his labors (he put in 32 years of continuously refurbishing and maintaining the halfway house to its present condition). If anything he was against any fanfare. He was there to help men become sober. His belief was to keep the weekly payments the same, for men who came into the Halfway house, and never to effect an increase.

Over the past 32 years, hundreds of men have gone through

this house and out of that group, hundreds have turned their lives around to sober living. Certainly, Harold Richards did deserve credit for starting a non-profit recovery home for men to overcome. The house has always been a big stepping stone for the sake of helping men recover from addiction, therefore why not create a special tribute to a man who has always been a giver and not a taker.

I shared my idea with my close friend, who was still alive, Mr. Frank Ivanovich, and was the former Treasurer of the Newport Mesa Halfway House and continued in the same capacity as treasurer with the new "Harold & Justine Richards Foundation." In my opinion the credit goes to Frank, because it was he who took the idea of the plaque one step further and turned it into a bust. All of this came to fullness while Frank and I were having coffee at my home. Mr. Ivanovich happened to notice a bust of the late tenor singer Mario Lanza sitting on my stereo equipment in my Gmmy Radio Studio. Frank then suggested that the bust for Mr. Richards sould be much better, bigger and made of metal, whereas the Mario Lanza bust was not made from metal and was much smaller. Frank had asked if he could borrow the Mario Lanza bust to take to an upcoming monthly committee meeting and display it before his fellow committee members. According to Frank, the committee members voted overwhelmingly for a bust to be created.

From that point on, one of the committee members took it another step further and introduced the idea to the present creator of the bust, sculptor Karen Schmidt (who did a marvelous job of creating the look alike bust of Harold Richards.) Today that bust is in the house and now sits upon a beautiful pedestal created by the talents of a carpenter of the Costa Mesa, California area.

On Saturday June 9, 2007 a special unveiling of the bust took place, with approximately 40 to 50 people attending, to pay homage to founder Mr. Harold W. Richards of the former "Newport Mesa Halfway House." which is now the new "Harold & Justine Richards Foundation."

The man who originally came up with the idea of the bust, who received the committee approval - Mr. Frank Ivanovich - was well loved by everyone who knew him including yours truly. He was my roadway to sobriety. Harold, Frank and I, were named the "Mount Rushmore Trio." We spent many weeks dining together. When these two gentlemen passed away I will always remember them for all they did for helping me and hundreds more to become sober. In Harold's words: "What You See Is What You Get." Those very same words are listed on the bust and in my heart as well.

Pictured from left: Frank E. Dee, With Harold Richards, Treasurer Frank Ivanovich, and Mike Mac Cormack. Harold Richards was the Owner of The Newport Mesa Halfway House which became The "Harold & Justine Foundation House".

L-R: Frankie Ivanovich, known as the Count, Mike Mac, Frankie Dee, and Harold the owner of the Halfway House. Harold, Frank and Mike devoted their life in helping new comers gain spiritual growth. Both Harold and Frank the Count Have passed on. I shall never forget them.

Interviewing Joey Bishop

In the late 1990's I had the honor of being invited to the home of Joey Bishop - one of the last members of the "Rat Pack." who lived in Newport Beach, California. I found him to be an easy-going gentleman who never had a bad word to say about people, places or things. Joey was really a down-to-earth, cool guy and never practiced using foul language. I asked him what it was like to be a member of the famed "Rat Pack?" He said it was composed of 100 percent clean cut members who didn't employ the use of curse words. Joey described member Dean Martin as another easygoing man who enjoyed entertaining audiences. Joey also claimed that Dean Martin knew how to confidently handle a horse with ease and could ride any horse when he starred in western movies.

I never enjoyed being around egotistical people, but when I was invited to Joey's home to meet him and his wife Sylvia, I didn't know what to really expect - meeting a super star of films, stage and night clubs, and a part time host of the Johnny Carson Tonight show. What I found were two humble down-to Earth entertainment giants. Through my first meeting, Joey Bishop and I quickly became friends. Joey would often call me to see how I was doing or invite me to his home to view some of the shows he performed with rat pack members Frank Sinatra, Dean Martin and Sammy Davis. Jr.

Joey Bishop was a quality comedian and without any doubt he has been regarded for his high standard of clean humor. He always avoided harmful ethnic jokes, and he never told "sick jokes." I have to honestly report to everyone that Joey Bishop was always very nice to yours truly. He often told me "my doors are always open to you."

When I asked him why he no longer continued to appear in clubs or on television shows, his answer was quite simple, "I've done it all, and it was time to retire."

I regularly received invitations to his home. However, I was too wrapped up in creating recovery meetings or managing the publication of my monthly American Liberty News which occupied much of my time, however, I'll never forget Joey Bishop. Thank you Joey Bishop for being a friend and patronizing my past American Liberty News magazine.

Joey Bishop was born February 3, 1918 in the Bronx. New York. He passed away October 17, 2007 at the age of 89. His wife Sylvia passed away in 1990 from cancer.

Joey and Sylvia Bishop

An Invitation To Warner Brothers Studios

I was honored to meet Jim Cornick, who became everyone's friend and who attended some of the meetings that I began in the early 90's. At the time, I did not know who he was or what he did. As a matter of fact, I have never been one to be a so-called 'nosey rosy guy' interested in everyone's personal business. As I got to know Jim through the sharing of positive topics - not only at my meetings - but what he shared with other groups about the spiritual topics of living life daily with God and living a clean, sober life without the booze. Jim always received superb applause from the groups attending the meetings. What he shared with others on the topic of living in sobriety were terrific, and after each meeting he would chat with various people and never once did he brag about his employment at Warner Bros. as a foreman in the Warner sound department. I re-named my new, but now old friend, "Hollywood Jim" of Warner Bros.

In the early 1990's, I had started a monthly political newsletter, in partnership with Mr. Warren Marsh who owned his own print shop. At that time, Jim wanted to donate a political monthly column in my newsletter. He asked me to select a title name for his column. I came up with the title "As Hollywood Jim Sees It Today, and Tomorrow." It blew his mind with laughter, and his column took off like a blaze of fire, mostly from readers who loved his political views. In his earlier career, Jim was also a noted writer for theater writing for the legitimate stage. This led him to a career working for Warner Bros. Studio and he was employed there for 30 years or so. Being politically motivated, he began writing for my American Liberty News Magazine. For each monthly issue, Jim took a stack of American Liberty News to his job site to pass out to workers and friends. In the meantime, Hollywood Jim also wrote two books, one in 1994 and another in 2003, and I have to state that I passed on reading both.

After attending one of my Wednesday night meetings Hollywood Jim approached asked if me and a friend, Frank, known as 'The Count' would be interested in attending a recovery meeting In one of the rooms at the Warner Bros. studios. We were in total shock to be invited to go to the great motion picture studio for a recovery meeting - which was about an hour's drive. At the freeway parking lot we approached by a Security guard, who asked whom would we be visiting. When I mentioned Hollywood Jim, the guard was quick to respond "oh you two guys are the drunks that Jim Cornick is expecting." We were not aware that Jim was in a small open vehicle hiding behind the guard's shed, laughing from what the guard had said to us. Otherwise, I had to admit it was a magnificent spiritual meeting with an attendance of 15 men and women. My friend Frank 'The Count' and I were awarded two beautiful white sweatshirts with the Warner Bros. logo design on the front. That shirt remains hanging in my closet to this day.

When word got out to attendees in some of our local weekly meetings that we were invited to Warner Bros. Studios to attend a recovery meeting, there were members who were lined up hoping to attend one of those meetings hosted by Hollywood Jim Cornick. And, no kidding, there were many guys and gals who wanted to be invited to the popular studio. From then on a group of us would get to attend a monthly meeting there when Hollywood Jim invited us. At those meetings they offered fresh coffee cakes, donuts and pastries. The Welcome Warner Mat was a rare treat for us. After all, when does one get invited to a well-known Hollywood studio to share their personal feelings on keeping sober.

Me and Jim Cornick

Memories Of Buddy Clark
Part From A 12 Year Old Boy

I was 12 years old when I first heard Buddy Clark's voice at a local neighbor's house on a wind-up RCA 'Victrola' - that was 1946. The song I heard him sing on the old breakable record disc was *Linda*. At the time, this song was a number one hit on all the music charts, and it was sweeping the nation. It seemed everywhere I went as a boy, everyone would be humming or singing to themselves that song, and many a parent were naming their newborn daughter, Linda.

The local neighbor had a large collection of Buddy Clark recordings, and he would play them for hours at a time. The Clark voice became part of the neighborhood. I remember very clearly that neighbor telling us young local boys of the neighborhood, how he grew-up in the west end of Boston with Buddy Clark, and how he went to school with him. I was so inspired by the stories about Buddy. Buddy became my so-called first mentor in music, as well as numerous other singers such as Mario Lanza, Perry Como, Al Martino, who came later in the early 50's. I wanted to sing just like them. I remember going home and trying to imitate the melodious Buddy Clark's tremolo sweet sound that he projected. Buddy Clark was my first vocal teacher and musical inspiration. Years later, singers Mario Lanza and Al Martino inspired me to begin vocal lessons. I entered a singing contest, and was amazed that I won first prize, grabbing the large sum of $5.00.

Buddy Clark became my stepping stone to the good music of that era. He was famous in the 30's and 40's. Buddy was known as a voice of romantics. But suddenly tragedy hit the nation. Buddy Clark died in an untimely plane crash on October 2, 1949. Bostonians, and yours truly, along with the rest of the nation, were in shock. One of the best crooners was gone. After this his recordings were being aired on radio for months, and even now, 65 years later. In the 50's Buddy Clark was well remembered. His recordings could be heard on various radio stations, and his songs can still be purchased on tape and CD's today.

It seems as one door in life closes for one singing super star, another one opens. In October of 1949 another new door was opened for new singing sensation Mario Lanza. He was now the new kid on the block and singing his way into the hearts of millions, through his new hit movie "The Midnight Kiss." His hit recording of "Be My Love" sold like hot cakes. Strange as it may seem, when I went to the Boston Public Library to look into the back archive copies of the Boston papers, I found Buddy Clark's story on his career and his death. On the very next page a new singer was being introduced to the public in the movie "The Midnight Kiss." He was Mario Lanza. The date of this paper I was looking at was October 3, 1949. Strange indeed. Buddy Clark and Mario Lanza both died on the same month in October. Clark died October 2, 1949, and Mario Lanza died October 7, 1959, ten years and five days after Buddy Clark's death, and Al Martino also passed away in October

Yes, in the highly charged and intensely exciting world of good popular M-U-S-I-C of the 1930's and the 40's, let us never forget the 50's, and some of the 60's - Buddy Clark, without doubt occupied a special place in the hearts of millions of people who knew and loved Buddy Clark's melodious baritone sound which this great singer delivered into our lives. You bet I became a big fan! He brought the romantics, the love, the memories to those of us who felt and knew his unique sounding voice. Buddy Clark's voice still continues to be heard often on certain radio stations around the United States, who continue to play good solid popular music of the golden days of yesteryear. Songs of easy listening with a touch of love will live with those of us who remember the giants of the vocals during the big band era, and we, who will continue to enjoy the good sounds of popular music, we play on GMMY RADIO daily.

Listed are only a few of the songs Buddy Clark turned into smash hits, which now may be purchased either on tape cassette, or CD, at your favorite music store, from Columbia Records.

Buddy Clark 16 Most Requested Songs

1. "I'll Dance At Your Wedding"
2. "Linda"
3. "How Are Things In Glocca Morra?"
4. "Ballerina"
5. "Peg O' My Heart"
6. "Love Somebody" (duet with Doris Day)

7. "Rosalie"
8. "Girl Of My Dreams"
9. "South America - Take It Away!"
10. "Now Is The Hour"
11. "My Darling, My Darling" (duet with Doris Day)
12. "It's A Big Wide Wonderful World We Live In"
13. "You're Breaking My Heart"
14. "A Dreamer's Holiday"
15. "Baby It's Cold Outside" (duet with Dinah Shore)

and here are some more favorites:
16. 'I'll Get By (As Long As I Have You)"
17. "If You Were Only Mine"
18. "I Still Get A Thrill"
19. "The Very Thought Of You"
20. "Stay As Sweet As You Are"
21. "It Had To BeYou"
22. "Sleepy Time Gal"

I may add one of my favorite Buddy classic songs he sang, and sang it so well, was 'I'm All Dressed Up With A Broken Heart.'

Years later, in the 50's came another great vocalist. A singer of the people, Jerry Vale, who honored Buddy Clark, with a beautiful album of Buddy's songs titled: "I Remember Buddy." This is one album you must add to your collection. Jerry Vale does an outstanding job in delivering these beautiful ballads. His rendition of "All Dressed-Up With A Broken Heart" is indeed magnificent. But then again so are all the songs Vale sings.

Recently, in 2014, Mr. Casey Wynstok from Los Angeles, donated the original first cut recordings of Buddy Clark's record inserted in leather books with Buddy's name printed in gold. Thank you Casey for all you did.

Buddy Clark

Al Martino and other Singers
Inspired Me to Take Voice Lessons

Although it has been a known fact that Mario Lanza had been a great inspiration to many singers as well as myself, it was Al Martino, who really inspired me to take voice lessons at the age of 15. When Al Martino's recording of "Here In My Heart" hit the radio airwaves of Boston, this great masterpiece also became a juke box favorite in our local hang-out called "The Teele Square Sweet Shoppee." (The spelling of 'Shoppee is exactly how it was spelled on the sign of the establishment). People would be greeted by Al's voice as it filled the square. The old gathering spot, "The Teele Square Sweet Shoppes" is now gone. But the memories of Al Martino's song "Here In My Heart" brought many a couple together.

L-R: Steve Lawrence, Eddie Fisher, DJ Brad Phillips, Al Martino and Dick Haymes

I can remember sitting in different booths wherever space was available while everyone would be taking turns to put their twenty five cents into the little juke box song selector that hung on the walls of whatever booth you sat, where you could make a selection of your favorite song. In those days for five cents you could listen to a wide selection of songs. The store owner John Abbott, was going out of his mind because everyone constantly played Al's record. The Wurlitzer juke box company was forever sending someone out to replace Al's recording of "Here in My Heart" worn out by being over-played. But it never stopped us adults who would come in for a ten cent cup of coffee or a twenty five cent ice cream Sundae or cheeseburger.

Old John Abbott, God Bless him, being a senior at the time, figured he could get us teens to stop playing Al's recording all night long, by insisting that we either had to buy a twenty cents shake or a sundae or a twenty five cents hamburger. But old John's plan never worked. Price change or whatever we kept on playing Al's recording, while John made extra money. I finally got the nerve to walk up to Mr. Abbott to ask him: "Don't you like Al Martino's song and his singing?" He replied: "I love Al Martino's voice, but not 24 hours of the day." It became a losing battle for old John. He finally dropped his prices back, and went along with Al being a favorite star in his Sweet Shoppee.

Everyone in those days was asking questions about Al Martino. 'Who is he'? 'What does he look like'? 'Where did he come from'? Nobody seemed to know, unless you were lucky enough to hear your favorite Disc Jockey introduce Al's recording and hear him talk about Al's background. Al's recording was selling like hotcakes at our local music store. You had to put an order in and reserve your '78' recording of "Here in My Heart." Many of us went to purchase Al's hit song only to find out that they were all sold out. The proprietor was taking reservations to hold a copy for the numerous consumers who were waiting to buy. When an additional batch of "Here in My Heart" came into the music store, the proprietor would hold the recording for those whose names were on the reservation list. That was how fast "Here in My Heart" was selling.

When I finally bought my recording, I drove my parents crazy by playing it over and over. I would sing along with Al, and it was because of Al's beautiful voice and this recording, that I decided to take voice lessons with a good Italian teacher who graduated from the same school at the same time the famous opera tenor Beniamino Gigli did. She was a great teacher of the 'Bel Canto' method of singing. While taking voice lessons I finally bought the music sheet for the large sum of forty cents. In those days sixty cents was a lot of money, and voice lessons cost three big bucks once a week, because that was all I could afford. I wanted to sing "Here in My Heart" for my practice song with my vocal teacher. But she made that song number two on her list. She insisted I learn "Sorrento" first. She was a strict vocal teacher, who insisted on her pupils learning Solfego and doing vocal Italian exercises. The singing of any song with her came with the later part of my vocal lesson.

I sang "Here In My Heart" for the first time in public in the key of b-flat at an Italian wedding at the Hotel Continental, in Cambridge, Massachusetts, and received a standing ovation from all the family, and friends who were invited. After that first scary event, of my singing "Here In My Heart" it became my opening song, due to the great response I received. I found myself singing in local pubs on weekends for five to seven dollars a night. Although I never pursued the career as a singer I did do musical comedy shows, while working at a regular job because I really liked clean humor.

But to this day it was Al Martino who really inspired me to study voice. Every now and then I will pull out of my treasure chest of songs one of Al Martino's first albums titled "The Exciting Voice Of Al Martino." On this album you hear the great quality of this man's voice. He doesn't belt out a song. He sings it out. This album contained such great songs as: "Here In My Heart," "Because You're Mine," "Granada," "The Loveliest Night Of The Year," "Nessun Dorma," "Exodus," "Mattinata," "Just Say I Love Her," "Non Ti Scordar Di Me," "Make Me Believe," "No More, Love," "Where Are You Now."

My good friend Bob Dolfi, my colleague and a great friend of the GMMY website stated he did not know that Al sang such beautiful songs as "NESSUN DORMA" an aria from Puccini's "Turandot." WOW! Al does a fantastic job on this aria as well as all the songs in this album. A few of my favorite songs in addition to "Here In My Heart," that Al sings on this album, are "Make Me Believe," and "No More." This album is one of many dynamic albums from Al. Years later Al Martino was a featured vocalist on my radio show. Needless to say I was honored to have him on my show as a telephone guest.

If I'm not mistaken, and I could very well be wrong. I remember as a 17 year old kid, that Al Martino was to appear at one of Boston's biggest night clubs called: "Blinstrubs." I remember I could not afford to go and that just about tore me apart.

At local record hops in those days, we would dance to Al's songs, and I can remember we would all applaud after each song he sang. But most of the applause went to Al's "Here in My Heart." Al was so popular with his first hit, that all the boys in the gang would play his record in the juke boxes, and then mouth the words and do gestures as though they were singing the song themselves. Poor old John Abbott would shake his head at those of us who would mouth the words while Al Martino sang.

Now in the year of 2015, I often wondered what John Abbott would have thought, if he were to hear "RAP" music? I think he would have had a stroke! And so folks you can thank God today that we had such a great singer and other popular vocalist of the 50's era, who provided us the best in music, and not in N-O-I-S-E-! Amen!

I'm only sorry that as a former manager of a weekly newspaper for 16 years, that I never had the opportunity to meet Mr. Martino in person, even though I did write articles about him and was proud to feature him on my radio show.

In closing as I used to say as I learned from my radio mentor Bill Marlowe: "Keep the sound down and the sunny side up, I'm the keeper of this recorded caper." Keep on digging Al Martino, for they don't come any better than this impeccable vocalist.

Al Martino and Frankie Dee

A Devoted Al Martino Fan
Frank Alia From Wisconsin

Frank Alia, who hails from Pleasant Prairie, Wisconsin, has always been proud to admit that he has been a fan of Al Martino ever since Al Martino first hit the radio air waves with his first hit song, "Here In My Heart." Alia, has not stopped his loyalty in being a great supporting fan of Al Martino's. Frank, proudly displayed Al Martino's autographed picture from Al Martino, which hangs on Alia's home wall.

"Al Martino, has always been one of my favorite singers, ever since he recorded his first hit song" said Alia. "How can rap or rock noise compare to such great singers as Al Martino? No way "commented Frank Alia.

Damon Lanza [center] takes a break from book signing to talk to Frank Alia and his wife Nina who are relatives to owner of the Salute restaurant. There were lines waiting to come into the Salute Restaurant to purchase the Biography book of Damon's father Mario Lanza. Note the photos of Mario Lanza on the walls of the restaurant.

Frank Alia's brother John and his wife Ida, are the proprietors of the popular Italian restaurant, "Salute" located on Main Street in Racine, Wisconsin. They also have posted an autographed photo of Al Martino on their restaurant wall. Upon entering the "Salute" Restaurant, one can be greeted by the songs of Al Martino where they often stop to view the autographed photo of Al Martino.

Frank's, lovely wife Nina, is a unique Italian chef, who has numerous recipes titled under "Nina's Cugina,"[Nina's kitchen] is also a fan of Martino's. Both Frank and Nina have often attended the Al Martino concert at the Milwaukee Italian Festival in Wisconsin. Frank Alia: "I'd even go all the way to Chicago to see Al Martino perform in person."

"The elder residents of Kenosha, Wisconsin never forgot the great sounds of the pop singers of the 40's and 50's, and there are some restaurants who still feature the good old juke boxes filled with the songs we all love" said Frank Alia.

Popular singer Al Martino takes time to meet fans Frank Alia and his wife Nina with their grandson Josh Alia at the Italian Milwaukee Festival. Al Martino appeared to a record breaking audience at the Milwaukee Italian Festival back in the early 2000's.

Kitty Kallen, Reminded Us That "Little Things Mean A Lot"

In 1954, kitty kallen was voted the most popular female singer in the USA according to Billboard and Variety.

The lyrics were so stunning and meaningful to the ears of us teens, because of the kindness and love we shared and gave to friends we dated through clean friendships and the things we said to help one another - you could really and honestly say, little things really did mean a lot. Who could ever forget the beautiful and unique voice of Kitty Kallen, which charmed the hearts of millions of

American audiences with that first hit solo. The good ole juke box never stopped playing it and even the adults of our day loved this lady's singing. There seemed to always be a line of people standing in front of the ole Juke box just to hear pretty Kitty's hit song.

Little things really did mean a lot to all of us, especially because of the beautiful lyrics - it was absolutely the most appropriate title for a song. The words and music were written by Edith Lindeman and Carl Stutz, and in 1954 the sheet music sold for fifty cents Are you ready for this? Yup! 50 cents. Try buying a song sheet at that price today. I still have the original song sheet that I purchased in 1954. That's over 60 years ago. It was indeed a plush song sang ever so well by Miss Kallen, who came up through the ranks as a child star that sang with the best of the big bands including Jimmy Dorsey, Harry James and Artie Shaw.

When I was a radio host back in the 1970's, at WHET, Boston, I pretty well wore-out Miss Kallen's 78's, "If I give My Heart to You," and "In the Chapel in the Moonlight," and "Besame Mucho." What charisma, what charm, and what a beautiful delivery she possessed. When she sang these songs she not only made our goose bumps stand-up like little musical soldiers, but she brought fond memories of love into our hearts, and if you happened to have been in a relationship at the time, especially when these two great hit songs were aired, you're sure to remember the closeness they brought into your relationship. Her songs were truly tear jerkers filled with nostalgic memories. I am honored to remind our listeners that Ms. Kitty Kallen's songs are still being featured on GMMY RADIO by all of the Gmmy Radio Hosts in this day of 2015.

Miss Kallen now lives in Mexico, she was formerly living in New Jersey.

Argeo Cellucci Jr: A Political Diplomat of Massachusetts Who Helped Everyone

Looking back into the 60's and early 70's, I had only wished the author of the musical stars, Mr. Richard Grudens, had met Argeo Cellucci Jr. from Hudson, Mass. Mr. Cellucci would have certainly invited Richard Grudens and his lovely wife Madeline to come to the Boston State house to meet his son Governor Paul Cellucci and have the news media take photos of Mr. and Mrs. Grudens.

Hudson, Mass: Behind every successful son or daughter who has established themselves in a career, are a father and mother who have groomed their children into becoming prosperous, decent human beings. Webster's Dictionary defines the word decent as: proper and fitting, respectable, adequate, fair and kind. This was Argeo R. Cellucci Jr. and his wife Priscilla who was a very giving Lady.

In a small town 40 or 50 miles West of Boston, Massachusetts is a town named Hudson. This is the town in which Argeo R. Cellucci Jr., and his wife Priscilla were born, raised, and married. They were the proud parents of Massachusetts Governor, Paul Cellucci who became the Ambassador to Canada. His father Argeo R. Cellucci Jr., was the town's Industrial Commissioner who for more years than I can remember devoted his life to turning Hudson into a prosperous, industrial, booming town. He helped everyone who needed help. The man was a spiritual human being who worked very hard luring favorable industry to the town of Hudson.

Mr. Cellucci wore many talented hats in his teen years, and once had his own band, played the saxophone, and also sang all the golden oldie songs of the 40's and 50's. In his late 60s and 70s, he continued to sing at invited parties and functions for his own pleasure, that included the annual dances I started every year and sponsored by the weekly News Enterprise paper owned by Mr. Earle W. Tuttle, my former boss. The money we made from the dances was given to the needy.

I remember asking Mr. Cellucci who his favorite singers were. He was quick to state "you don't have enough paper to write down all the great singers I adored but here's a few: Don Cornell,

Jerry Vale, Al Martino, Mario Lanza. He also loved the sound of the Big Bands of the 40's and 50's. Argeo Cellucci Jr., was a casual, easy going spiritual human being who had so much consideration for his fellow man. The casual Argeo R. Cellucci Jr., was known by friends and the town's people of Hudson as "Junior."

However, not enough was said about the trials and tribulations Argeo has lived through to make Hudson prosperous in his works as Commissioner and as a businessman. Behind every successful, married, business man is a foundation of love, strength, understanding, and compassion. His love, and understanding came from his wife, Priscilla Cellucci, who deserved much credit for "Junior's" success. Priscilla, without a doubt was one of the finest ladies, with integrity, honesty, and is to be commended not only as a wife, and a mother but also a good friend to her husband and the people of the town of Hudson. She had shared her support and understanding, when "Junior" needed such support to achieve his goals, Priscilla was always there for her husband. Her goals were simple: sincerity, honesty and good family values. What was Priscilla Cellucci like? She was brilliant, well educated, very congenial and down to earth. Governor Paul Cellucci served as Lt. Governor for two terms after being overwhelmingly voted in as the Governor in 1998. Paul Cellucci, has been elected to many political offices. He has never been defeated, beginning as a town Selectman to State Rep to State Senator, to Lt. Governor, and Governor.

Argeo Cellucci Jr, a retired prominent business man who continues to be a diplomat in local and state politics, never forgot his roots growing-up in days when times were tough. He enjoys helping people whenever possible. Without any doubt Mr. Cellucci was a people's person who will go to any length to help all walks of life be they poor, or elite. I certainly know this to be true. He was like a brother to me and often time came to my home for a home-made Italian pasta dinner. He was a very spiritual human being who carried a photo in his shirt pocket of Our Lord Jesus Christ.

Argeo Cellucci Jr, was President of the United States Oldsmobile dealership, and often time would visit out of state Oldsmobile dealers. I always remembered designing some of his full page advertisements for our newspaper Beacon publications, for whom I worked.

His contribution to good music was to "Proclaim Mario Lanza

Day" on October 7, 1999, in which a special proclamation was issued from the Governor's office, for the late tenor Mario Lanza. Mr.
Cellucci, also shared tribute to Lanza as a specially invited guest
on the popular Ron Della Chiesa radio show at WGBH FM radio in
Boston.

Argeo, Me and Paul Cellucci

Argeo and Me

Argeo and Me above and below.

Meeting Jerry Vale
At The Blue Moon In Lowell, MA

Jerry Vale, a very popular singer was booked at the Blue Moon in Lowell, Massachusetts. It was a Saturday night and the night club was not well attended for the first show. I remember this so clearly. We had made reservations for front row tables. How delighted we were to be able to see and hear Jerry Vale in person for the very first time. That evening Jerry wore a black Tux (he always did) and in those days Jerry was no silver fox. None of us were until the old hair had turned to silver or white if you like.

Jerry's opening song "I'm Sitting on Top of the World" was performed in a jump mode. He sang a number of refreshing songs that evening and he sang them so beautifully. His voice to my ears sounded smooth and velvety, full of Jerry's famous rich tones, a melancholy and exuberant sensuality sung and delivered roman-tically, that's the only way I could describe Jerry Vale's voice. But being Italian, the songs I loved and enjoyed the most were: "Sor-rento," "Mama," "O Sole O Mio," and "Mala Femmina." Vale brought the house down with applause from young and old alike that very evening and I was whistling and applauding like a teenager.

When the first show ended, my date asked if it would be possible if we could meet Jerry Vale for his autograph. I had no problem walking over to the other side of the nightclub room where Mr. Vale was standing and asking him for his autograph. I told him that my date wanted to meet him as well. Unbeknownst to me, not only did Jerry Vale give us his autograph, but was very casual, and allowed us to ask him questions. He even asked us to remain for the second show, and he also danced with the girl I had dated.

At that time, I remember asking his manager, Paul Insetta, why hasn't Jerry recorded the two songs: "Mama," and "Sorrento?" The reply I received was: "Those songs wouldn't go over." Not too long afterwards a new upcoming female singer, Connie Francis, recorded "Mama," which earned her a big hit on the charts, and a gold record. I had often wondered what Jerry Vale's later thoughts were on this?

Meeting Jerry Vale For The Second Time

I became a Jerry Vale fan and followed his appearances whenever he appeared in the Boston area. In one particular night club, Jerry made his mark as one of the best singers to ever appear (at the Frolics night club in Revere, Mass. - which is no longer in operation). The Frolics was known by those of us who would attend Jerry's show regularly, as Jerry Vale's second home, because he was always in demand with audiences and booked there more than most entertainers. The owner of that club was Chicky Della Russo, who was related to a close friend of mine at the time.

I had been studying voice way before Jerry Vale became popular. On one particular Saturday night a group of vocal students of mine were studying opera with my same voice teacher. This group of vocal students who had never seen the inside of a night club, even if they fell over the doorsteps, decided to attend with your's truly, to see and hear Jerry perform. The remarks made by these so called opera buffs that evening after Jerry finished his performance were "This Vale guy sings with beautiful placed 'Belcanto' tones. He truly does sing with ease, placement and with a great delivery."

From that time forth, my student friends and I would make it a practice that every time Jerry would appear at the Frolics, we would all attend. In the late 50's when Jerry was starring at the Frolics, he was doing two shows a night. One on the roof top, and the other in the main club room below. Jerry packed this club with an unbelievable wall-to-wall audience. If you wanted to see Jerry perform at this club, you had to have reservations weeks ahead of time.

Jerry's Records Were Played At Intermission

In my teens, I was learning, as an apprentice, to be a movie projectionist in our local theater. I would always play Jerry's recordings of the old 78's, during Intermission before the movie would start. The theater audience would applaud after each of Jerry's records that were played.

Back To Radio

In the 70's, word got around the radio circuit that Jerry Vale had lost his voice, and disappeared from performing. It's amazing how uncalled rumors start. I never liked getting into anyon'e personal life, namely because it's not my business and it shouldn't be anyone else's! But no one should go by hearsay. Hearsay destroys! On my radio show, Vale was a great artist to all of us who enjoyed what he gave us. Jerry was a great voice and sang great songs and I'll add that he was a great man of song! And this is what I knew about Jerry Vale. He perhaps forgot about that little teenage eighteen year old kid, and with all the autographs he signed and people he met. But I never forgot him.

Jerry Vale and
Richard Grudens

I featured Jerry Vale's songs on my radio show and there were two recordings that were my favorites: "I'm All Dressed Up with a Broken Heart," and "You Are Always in My Heart." I felt for years that these songs were sung so brilliantly only by Jerry. He sang the most meaningful lyrics that have ever been put into a song. During my years in radio, and playing the kind of good music

I loved and featured on my show from big bands to big name popular vocalists, I always avoided entertainers with an ego. I associated myself with those who had humility. I regret that I never did get the chance to have Jerry on my show, because perhaps times had already changed when radio went to rock, and the station [WHET] from where I hosted my show, was about the last one to continue playing the good stuff of the 50's. I often wondered if he would have remembered me from the Blue Moon or the Frolics in Revere Beach, Mass? I'll never really know. Thank you Jerry Vale for all your wonderful songs you sang for all of us.

Jay Orlando - Super Star of the Sax

I first met Jay Orlando about 30 years ago in the Union Plaza which was a Las Vegas Casino where he performed for three years the good sounds of music from the 40's through the 60's. Jay Orlando appeared at 2000 shows at the Union Plaza six days a week. He became the popular saxophonist of the Las Vegas casinos and clubs. In a recent chat with my good friend Jay, he stated his appearances were at the popular casinos such as the Freemont and the The Silver Slipper which are now gone. It was really a delight to chat with him about the good old days in Vegas.

Jay always played the 'good stuff' as I called it and his style of good music was the way of life for a jazz artist and pop musician such as Jay. He could play any song title starting with any letter from the alphabet from A to Z - he was indeed sensational.

I created a website in Jay's honor for free and please allow me to explain that it wasn't about making a profit. Gmmy websites and Gmmy Radio never charge anyone to go on line, Gmmy is strictly a labor of love to promote good musicians and keep the music flowing from great musical artists such as Jay Orlando. For those who wish to purchase some of Jay's CD's all you have to do is contact Jay Orlando on his website on Golden Music Memories Of Yesteryear at this URL listed below.

Please read the below article, which is on Jay Orlando's website.

http://www.gmmy.com/bands/Jaybio.htm

"The Sexiest Sax In Show Biz"

That's how saxophone virtuoso Jay Orlando is known to his legion of fans. And he can be counted on to live up this billing at every performance. Orlando, who has always had a mystical faith in his ability to weave sheer musical magic with his golden sax, has become the high priest of the instrument.

Jay does with the sax what Tom Jones and Elvis Presley did with a song - frenetic body gyrations and all. The whole atmosphere of the room is charged with electric excitement the minute his sax goes into action. Crowds flood the immediate area, whooping it up in a heavenly frenzy that would create havoc at an African voodoo convention.

Orlando's sax sexiness isn't his only musical trademark. A true aura of saxophobia pervades any room offering his electrifying wares. He's richly endowed with superb tone and flawless technique. His mass appeal, unique musical styling, extraordinarily dextrous playing, creativity, magnetic personality, and impeccable musicianship readily communicate themselves to his rapt listeners.

It's no wonder then that ORLANDO'S sensational sax work, featuring great individuality and tremendous lift, has been likened to the legendary instrumental soloists of the big band era - musical giants who spellbound their audiences with their powerhouse performances. Jay happens to be the hardest working instrumentalist in the world of music. Gifted with an incredibly boundless supply of energy, his remarkable sounds are never muted throughout each of his action packed and thrill-studded shows.

His audiences, invariably keyed to a high state of excitement and explosive emotionalism, seemingly appear more exhausted than ORLANDO. Many shake their heads in disbelief at JAY'S sustained sax excursions and amazing bursts of energy - equivalent to a carload of tigers.

ORLANDO, who was born in Detroit, Michigan of Italian parentage, was hooked on music at an early age. While other kids on his block played baseball and stick ball and went swimming, Jay spent many enraptured hours listening to big band Detroit's Fox Theatre.

On many occasion he would use his school lunch money for a front seat view of the parade of bands at the Fox. Sometimes he would play hookey from school. Especially if the matinee show schedule conflicted with school hours. At the age of 13 his parents enrolled him in a music school conducted by Professor Anthony Peligrini. The good Professor thought all good Italian musical students should learn how to play the accordion. Jay's parents were persuaded to buy their son such an instrument against the angry protestation of the budding musician.

Orlando's opposition to the accordion made sense. He had

a burning desire to be a big band musician and had discovered that an accordion wouldn't do it for him.

It took Jay two years and many a knuckle - rapping from Peligrini's busy ruler before he won his point. Convinced that a saxophone rather than an accordion was the answer, the Orlando's bought one for their son.

At eighteen he was touring the country with bands and playing the top hotel rooms and night clubs. Concentrating on tenor sax, he played big - band swing, Dixieland dance music, country music, rock 'n' roll. And symphonic music. All this led to the formation of his first combo in 1956, the springboard for his meteoric career.

Note: Jay Orlando's Recordings are played on Gmmy Radio, for instructions on how to tune Into Gmmy Radio See Below. Visit Gmmy Radio at this URL - www.gmmy.com.

I was honored to have been invited to a special dinner that Kathryn Crosby had put on for me and my brothers when she and Tony appeared in the popular play "SAME TIME NEXT YEAR" in New Hampshire and Also in Cape Cod. Mass., in the 1970's. I saw this play two different times and when both of these two terrific actors appeared, they were sensational. Tony is my cousin and I owe him big time for what he did for me when I came to California. Tony loaned me $15,000 dollars to buy my first mobile home in California. In a month's time I paid off the loan to him when I closed my Boston Bank account. I was so grateful for all he did for me especially when I was drinking. When I got sober, he asked me to be his best man in June 1985.

He also did a play in Costa Mesa and for about 10 weeks he stayed at my home, it was a big honor to host him.

Tony Russo's wedding June 1985 in Las Vegas....I was his best man. From left Frankie is Toasting Tony and his wife Renee Russo, and far right is Terry Beeson my room mate. I was sober and enjoying a good life. The wedding cake melted due to it being 114 degrees and the air conditioner died due to an electric problem. Yikes!!!

Tony Russel and Me

Special Thanks To My Friend Terry Beeson

Thank you Terry for
all you did in helping
me to recover from
alcoholism, and thank
you for helping me in
my garden and with
the chores around the
house.

God Bless with love
and happiness and
good health.

I RECALL

Mario Lanza

Gmmy Website Created
A Lanza Legacy Website In 1999

Mario Lanza was one of the rarest tenors of our time. He was the hottest and biggest singing tenor sensation of the late 40's and 50's. And today his voice continues to grow in popularity with the new upcoming generation of opera fans. Mario Lanza, could sing Opera, Classical, and pop songs with ease in a vocal range that most tenors could not. Crowds swarmed him like bees wherever he performed, and his magnificent tenor voice was like a magnet, that drew people together. His voice brought goose bumps up and down the spines of audience's, and tears to many. As the late Bob

Dolfi said, "Mario Lanza continues to bring people together." Mario's powerful tenor voice was even known to have shattered a mirror at the home of columnist Hedda Hopper. Only close friends were aware Mario had heart problems, and high blood pressure. Mario Lanza's untimely death was caused by a third heart attack that shocked the world and millions of fans who loved him. Yet his magical tenor voice still continues to live with us all.

My colleague who has written many great articles and stories on Mario, never once believed that Mario was done in by the Mafia. One well-

Sketch of Mario Lanza

known writer, our good friend Joe Curreri said "I never once believed that Mario Lanza was murdered by the Mafia." On a past visit to Rome, Italy, to correct the lies, Damon Lanza and Bob Dolfi have proven that Mario had high blood pressure, and heart problems. They were told by the doctors in Rome that the third heart attack was the one that took Mario away from us. When Bob Dolfi published his book it was the gospel truth about Mario's passing. At the time of Mario's death, all the news papers across the nation stated that Mario's death was caused by ongoing heart problems, and at the time Mario Lanza also had the added complication of phlebitis

-- blood clots in the leg.

Mario Lanza's vocal techniques were natural and indeed God given. He could sing operatic roles when he was in his 20's that most tenors didn't attempt to sing until they were in their later years. Lanza was indeed a true icon among the tenors. There have been many books written on Mario's life in the past. The truthful facts among all books published about Lanza's death were truthfully printed in Bob Dolfi and Damon Lanza's book titled "Be My Love."

To the many fans, Gmmy Website created one of the biggest Mario Lanza websites in 1999 which is still on line for Lanza fans to visit: Golden Music Memories of Yesteryear website Ihad created with the help of Mike Roberts. Mike helped create our former magazine American Liberty News that continues to endorse all the fan clubs and newsletters through-out the world. Mario Lanza died on a Wednesday on October 7, 1959.

October 7, 2015 will mark the 56th year of Mario's death. In reality, Mario did not pass away. He is still with us musically. His glorious voice will continue to flow over the airwaves into the hearts of those who appreciate this God given voice that only belongs to Mario Lanza.

Damon Lanza

How I Met Damon Lanza And Bob Dolfi

Damon Lanza the, son of the legendary great tenor Mario Lanza, is perhaps one of the most easy going people I have ever met, one who has dedicated his entire life in promoting his father, Mario Lanza. I have had the honor of meeting Damon in the early 70's (via phone) when I was hosting my own radio show titled: "The Frank E. Dee Show" over radio station, W.H.E.T. (now defunct) in Waltham, Massachusetts. I was also managing a group of weekly newspapers in Acton, Massachusetts through Terry Robinson's nephew, who at the time was working as a printer for the same newspaper. He happened to read one of my articles on Mario Lanza's movie "Serenade" on which I wrote a review. He approached me asking if I would like to meet Terry's mother who was at that time living with Terry's brother. Of course I agreed, and was invited to his house to meet Terry's mother, who for hours on end told me the great stories of how wonderful a person was Mario and that she was like a second mother to Mario, who at one time lived in the household of Maria Lanza's mother. She had advised that they were real close friends.

Mrs. Robinson (Terry's mother) gave me the phone number and address of her son, whom I began to write letters, and soon was calling him on the phone. Terry offered Damon's phone number to me, and this was the beginning of how I got to meet Damon. In 1978, I moved out to California, and continued to remain in close touch with Damon. Damon had always been a congenial host and had invited me to his home in the Pacific Palisades, California, which was approximately 40 miles from where I live today. At that time Bob Dolfi had moved into his own apartment. He moved into Damon's house. I spent a number of weekends at Damon's house before Bob moved in. And as always there were nothing but barrels of laughs, good food, and good camaraderie. I was honored to have been invited for a Thanksgiving dinner, which was one of the best I ever enjoyed. Through Damon, and Marc Lanza, I was introduced to Bob, and that was the beginning of a good friendship with Bob Dolfi.

Damon, being a patriotic person, always celebrated the 4th of July at his home with friends. On many such occasions, there was always a wonderful party to which I was always invited, but never got to go due to work schedules.

Our friendship grew over the years, and at one time, the father of the Governor Paul Cellucci of Massachusetts, wanted to meet Damon. I remember calling him and if it would be possible to meet Mr. Argeo Cellucci Jr. (father of the Governor). Damon, without batting an eye, said "come on up as soon as you can." When we arrived at Damon's house I took pictures of Mr. Cellucci, Damon, and Terry Robinson who came over to Damon's house to meet Mr. Cellucci. Damon presented Mr. Cellucci with a LP recording and an eight track tape of Mario's Coca Cola show. Mr. Cellucci to this day has never forgotten the wonderful welcome that Damon had offered him and often reminds me of that great event.

In the early 80's, at one of my visits to Damon's house, Terry Robinson came by to say hello and brought the manuscript of his book, which was to be edited and published. He showed me the rough of the book, and asked me to give my opinion. At that time I thought it was great, because I was not aware of the truthful facts on Mario's death, until later years, when Bob Dolfi had corrected me. However, this article isn't about Terry, it's about Damon. Anyone who has met Damon Lanza will find that as tall as he is, so is his heart. He has always been a giving person, especially to his father's fans. Before Damon's death he regularly traveled worldwide visiting fan clubs in Europe and America and answering questions for fans, signing autographs, and having his picture taken with whoever asked. He always made each individual feel that he's known them a life time. His generosity was above and beyond most people who I have met who are in the so called limelight of showbiz. Damon was always a down to earth person caring man.

I was very fortunate to have friends like Bob Dolfi and Damon Lanza. We shared a common bond of knowing how to laugh and not take yourself too seriously. I enjoyed the clean humor that came from Damon Lanza. Thank you Damon for being a good close friend to all of us who knew you.

Most importantly, I thank Bob Dolfi, who enlightened me over the years on the truthful facts surrounding Mario Lanza. How gullible I could have been to have trusted others who were not truthful to me. We learn from our mistakes in trusting people who I honestly thought were truthful sincere and honest people. I have had the honor of meeting the son of a great tenor, Mario Lanza, and my good friend Bob Dolfi. Both men have passed on due to heart attacks.

Taking a luncheon break of Italian sandwiches at Lake Michigan in Kenosha. Wis.
L-R: Frankie Dee, Damon Lanza and Bob Dolfi

Preparing For Another Trip To The Salute Restaurant - L-R: Damon Lanza, Frank E. Dee and Bob Dolfi

Meeting Bob Dolfi & The Lanza Brothers

Bob Dolfi always promoted great legendary tenor Mario Lanza. Bob became a bigger fan after meeting Mario's parents. Bob was also from my home state of Massachusetts and from the same city of Somerville, Mass. Coincidentally, Bob also was a high school student of the same teacher I had in the elementary school in Somerville (Hodgkins). We never met until years later when we both moved to California. However, I got to meet Mario Lanza's sons' Marc and Damon in the late 70's. I was invited to spend a weekend up at the beautiful home Mario Lanza bought for his parents in Pacific Palisades, California, and I honestly have to admit I did some heavy drinking in those days. It was there that I first met Bob Dolfi who became close friends with Damon and Marc Lanza.

There was always a special welcome mat open for yours truly with plenty of humor and good food to enjoy with Damon, Marc Lanza and Bob Dolfi. It was there that I got to meet Terry Robinson who was Mario's physical trainer who kept Mario Lanza in good shape for the movies. I'll never forget Terry Robinson showing me the script of "Lanza His Tragic Life" before it became published in 1980. I was sitting in the living room when I was introduced to Terry Robison by Damon and Marc Lanza. Terry wanted an opinion of what I thought about his script about Mario Lanza's book soon to be published. My answer to Terry Robinson was simple, "I'm not one to give an opinion on something I don't know anything about."

However I being a Lanza fan was enthused to hear that a book on Mario Lanza was going to be published. Terry had told me he had to pull out some of the script because it was not up to par. [Whatever

Damon Lanza and Frankie Dee

that meant at that time].

I was really honored to have become good friends with Damon, Marc, and Colleen Lanza, and of course Bob Dolfi. There was a lot of tragedy in the Lanza Family. Marc Lanza passed away on 1991, I remember going to the services. On July 19, 1997 Colleen Lanza was struck by a car while crossing the street near her home, she died on August 4th at age 48. It was very sad to hear such devastating news. Colleen was a noted singer, and I can recall hearing her recording on Boston Radio, while I was living back there. Colleen was encouraged by her father's producer, Joe Pasternak, she had a short singing career while working with Lee Hazelwood, a protégé of Nancy Sinatra. Colleen's voice was considered harmonious and pleasant, however her career did not continue. Years later Damon Lanza passed away on 2008. Both Damon Lanza and Bob Dolfi started the Lanza Legend newsletter, whereas I did the first three layouts of the Lanza Legend publications by setting the type and page-make up for printing of the Lanza Legend. Bob and Damon also started the Lanza Legend website to keep the tenor Mario Lanza known. The website is www.lanzalegend.com

A sad time for yours truly when Bob Dolfi passed away from a heart attack on January 25, 2011. I will never forget you Bob always talking highly about author Richard Grudens's books. Bob Dolfi posted this wonderful tribute to Mr. Richard Grudens on our special website page tribute to

http://www.gmmy.com/crooners/RICHARD.htm

Mario Lanza Author Bob Dolfi Praises Richard Grudens

"Being somewhat of an author although not in Richard Grudens' class, I do know what to look for in a book. Sometimes it's not what you say as much as how you say it and Richard portrays this teaching very well in his books. It is so refreshing to read about a personality without having to sort through all the lies, innuendoes and smut before getting to the man himself. I commend Richard for being true to his subject as well as himself and it shows. Well done Richard."

A Special Biography Of An
Honest Friend - Bob Dolfi

He used to sing, and write, sculpt and cook, he was a connoisseur of good homemade Italian cooking and wines. He's been a successful businessman. He devoted a lifetime promoting Mario Lanza: this was Bob Dolfi.

As I mentioned previously, Bob and yours truly, came from the same city (back East) of Somerville, Massachusetts. We had the same teacher but in different years, and we lived approximately 4 to 5 miles from one-another, yet we never met until 1978 at the home of Damon and Marc Lanza. Bob attended school back in Somerville, from elementary to high school, when his father decided to move out of Massachusetts in the 1950's.

Bob reminisces about his Massachusetts junior high school teacher, the very same one I had as my 5th grade teacher. His name was James Develin. Bob said he was assigned a special back row desk next to the door, not for being smart. No, the desk was assigned to Bob so that the teacher could keep an eye on him, and besides Bob always wanted to be the first one out of the class. The very same seat Bob was assigned to was the desk of the late actor Richard Carlson of the popular TV Series: I Led Three Lives. And, as coincidences may be, and uncanny as it may sound, Mr. Develin also assigned me a back row seat in the 5th grade so he could keep an eye on me.

While living back east, Bob remembers when his dad would often take him to the old "Scolly Square" in Boston, where a famous burger and hot dog eatery was located. The famous burlesque theaters "The Casino" and "The Old Howard" were also located there, as well as the popular night club, the 'Crawford House" where the famous stripper Sally Keith, The Queen of the Tassels, was the star headliner for years. Before "Scolly Square" became the "John F. Kennedy Center," there was a famous hot dog & hamburger eatery called "Joe & Nemos," a landmark for its great hot dogs and burgers. There one could purchase a hot dog or hamburger for 10¢ each. Seemed everyone in Massachusetts would dine on their famous fare." They were open 24 hours a day.

How did Bob get to become a fan of Mario Lanza? It started in Somerville, Massachusetts. As the story was told to me while Bob was still living there. One day Bob was being punished by his parents for his pranks and naughtiness as is usual for a normal 14-year old boy, who was no different than most young teen boys coming from the tough streets of education. Bob's parents had sent him to his room on this particular day for being the so-called bad boy of the neighborhood. While Bob was in his bedroom, he turned on his radio, and heard a beautiful tenor voice flowing from the radio waves that filled Bob's room with what he said was the most beautiful voice he had ever heard in his life, and on radio. Bob said that Mario's voice sent tingles throughout his body, and that Mario's voice was full of magic and brought tears to his eyes. Bob was now hooked and became and instant fan of Mario Lanza's and one of his best and most supportive worldwide fans. He was so inspired that he took voice lessons and did perform during his early years in

Damon Lanza, Frankie Dee, Bob Dolfi

California. It was through one of his performances that Bob sang "I'll never Walk Alone" and had the honor of meeting Mario's parents for the first time. It was in the early 60's shortly after Mario's passing. Bob was thrilled and he became like another son to Mario's parents and a brother to the four Lanza children.

Bob spent countless days at the home of Mario's parents, Tony and Maria Cocozza. They loved Bob as though he was their own son and confided to Bob about Mario's personal life, his faults, his musical background, his schooling and his youthful days growing up in South Philadelphia, and much more. There wasn't anything unturned that Bob did not learn from Mario's parents about his favorite idol. There were intimate secrets that Tony and Maria would tell Bob that they never revealed to any of Mario's closest friends. There were Mario's friends who were not really liked by Tony. But that is another story, which one day may come to light.

Allow me to elaborate a little further about Bob Dolfi, his life and his successes. Bob has been in numerous successful business' ever since he first began a long career in the line of sculptors with his father in the early 1960's. His dad's business was located on Santa Monica Blvd in California. The name of the business was Van Neste, with Bob's father's name as the proprietor "Ossie Dolfi." The sculptor studio was well known with Hollywood studios and stars and with opera houses for creating difficult, detailed busts or whatever was required in the way of sculptures for use in Hollywood studios. Bob loved his father very much they were not just a father and son family team, but real close friends as well. Bob recalls in a humorous way, when he had told his father he was joining the U.S. Army, his father asked him why he wanted to enlist into the army, being so young. Bob retorted back in a serious manner "I DON'T HAVE ANYTHING BETTER TO DO." A real classic and humorous Bob Dolfi answer, and I still laugh thinking about that answer to his dad shaking his head as if to say, "I can't believe I just heard what I did" and walked away from his comical son. Bob had enlisted in the US Army for 3 years, an experience and adventure he never forgot. He was grateful to have served his country.

Through Bob's father's business, Bob now had become an artist in his own right and could create any type of sculpture. He met numerous actors for whom he created busts and whatever else they asked Bob to create. He became good friends with giants of the silver screen and rubbed elbows with many such great stars including John Wayne, Dean Martin, Rock Hudson, among many others.

Not only did Bob know how to sculpt, he became a noted

chef. He learned to cook by observing his mother's homemade Italian cooking. On many occasions, actor Rock Hudson would call Bob to come to his home and cook Italian dishes for the actor's parties. One evening Rock Hudson had called and asked Bob to come over and cook for a guest. The guest was none other than Doris Day. Bob agreed on one condition that he would cook for Rock Hudson if Rock had Doris sing one of her hit songs "Secret Love" for him. Doris was happy to fulfill Bob's request. Bob had told yours truly that Doris sang it so beautifully.

Bob was an adventurous person who was not afraid to take chances like going into the restaurant business, in which he was very successful. He even opened a fast-food restaurant in England. And that isn't all. He became a proud owner of his own winery in California where he sold the best imported and local California wines. In later years he and Damon Lanza and Marc Lanza, became owners of a few other restaurants, which also became successful for the threesome.

Marc Lanza and Frankie Dee

Bob has never forgotten his early roots in his early days in Somerville, Massachusetts, where he learned to work at an early age and be responsible for his actions. His goal is very, very, simple, "live in honesty, and publish the true facts." And this is what Bob Dolfi was all about.

After more than 36 years of Bob doing justice in keeping Mario Lanza's voice and his legacy alive, he continued to travel worldwide with Damon to various fan clubs and perform in trivia shows at his and Damon's own personal expense. There have been some people who have always thought Bob had his hand out via his association with Damon and Marc Lanza, which is a complete lie!! The truth of the matter is that Bob had always been self supporting through his own personal success and wealth. He never had to depend on anyone for his financial needs. Bob Dolfi was truly a self supporting man in all his affairs. There have been more times than anyone would really know, that Bob has more than picked up expenses, where Damon and Marc's family members never took the time to concern themselves.

Bob continued to carry the Mario Lanza Legacy, and correct the untruthful lies and rumors about his favorite hero. He made an honest commitment to Mario's parents that he would continue to expose the truth and go after those who have lied or distorted stories and rumors that were not truthful. Bob pulled no punches when he had to editorialize in the popular newsletter THE LANZA LEGEND, about the liars and wild rumors. He had even gone one step further in asking anyone who reads the Lanza Legend to dispute his comments. Since 1997 when the Lanza Legend was born, there has never been anyone who has yet come forth to disprove Bob's truthful facts. The goodness of Bob is that he did not back down from anyone. He was the kind of a real friend, who did take a truthful stand. And this is the Bob Dolfi I knew and still respect even after his passing.

I'll state that there has never been a truer friend than Bob Dolfi. I have seen over the past years all of the time he devoted in promoting Mario Lanza, and carrying the message out there to a younger generation. He would get up very early in the am and work through the day promoting Mario. And if by chance you do know someone who does what Bob did, I'll be the first to stand corrected.

There were those who were jealous of what Bob accomplished in his life time of carrying the Mario Lanza banner to every corner of this planet wherever there is a Mario Lanza Fan Club. Plus, you can still view Bob's past postings on Gmmy websites. And so I ask who else could do what he has done in keeping the Mario Lanza Legacy alive? A promise well kept to Mario's parents.

I have seen Bob, more times than I can count, going out on a limb to send people, at no charge, CD's or tapes of Mario Lanza. Bob was always the first in line to volunteer to send Mario's CD'S and cassettes and even photos and he never asked for one cent. In his own words he'd say "It's for Mario."

Robert "Bob" Dolfi passed away on January 25th, 2011 as a

result of heart failure at Torrance Memorial Hospital, CA. Bob was a close friend of the late tenor's parents, and of Lanza's sons Marc Lanza (died 1991) and Damon Lanza (died 2008). I had attended Marc Lanza's funeral, but missed Damon's.

Damon Lanza and Bob Dolfi founded the Lanza Legend, a newsletter and website devoted to keeping the name and voice of Mario Lanza alive. The newsletter is no longer being published. The website, lanzalegend.com, attracts readers and forum participants world-wide. Following the death of Damon Lanza, Bob continued the project in association with his wife Marlene and another Lanza authority, New Zealand broadcaster Lindsay Perigo. Bob was the principal author of Be My Love - A Celebration of Mario Lanza (1999- 2008) which included Damon Lanza, Perigo, singers Al Martino, Kathryn Grayson, Licia Albanese, Jose Carreras and Lanza biographers.

Damon Lanza, Kathryn Grayson and Bob Dolfi

A Special Tribute To Nick Petrella

The First President Of The Mario Lanza Institute And Museum - By Joe Curreri

Nicholas Petrella, 70, one of the original incorporaters of the Mario Lanza Institute And Museum and President for 30 years, died of cancer July 3rd, 1994. He was survived by brother Daniel, sister Marie, sister-in-laws Anne and Betty, nephews Louis and Thomas, and nieces, Elizabeth Plum and Margaret Skotnicki. Also his fiancée of 20 years, Frances Zirilli.

After 35 years as "South Philly's Record King," Nick Petrella retired his record business in 1985 and devoted himself full time as President of the non-profit institute to perpetuate the memory of world-famed tenor/actor Mario Lanza and to award Lanza Scholarship grants to young talented singers.

Joe Curreri

Even though he was born handicapped (use of his left arm), it didn't deter his fight for life. A graduate of South Philadelphia High School, he opened a record shop in 1946 on the corner of 19th and Mercy Streets. A few doors down, 2040 Mercy, lived a handsome young man named Alfredo Cocozza who changed Nick Petrella's life forever. That young man changed his name to Mario Lanza and startled the world with his magnificent voice.

A well-known and respected Community member with friends far and near, Petrella won many laurels including the "Mario Lanza Award" in 1967 and the "Christopher Columbus Award" in 1992.

In his early years, Nick became a promoter and his friends included the greats of show business: Al Martino, Fabian, Bobby Rydell, Buddy Greco. Jimmy Darren, even the Beatles, promoting their records and personal appearances at his record shop. His "Wall of Fame" included photos of him with all the stars including Mario Lanza, of course, and even Frank Sinatra and Dean Martin.

But the photo of him and Lanza was the most treasured. After moving his shop to Broad & Snyder, he opened a back room as a Mario Lanza Museum. In 1976, Mayor Frank Rizzo cut the ribbon at the opening ceremony.

His greatest memory came in 1949 when Mario Lanza returned to Philadelphia after making his first movie, "That Midnight Kiss." Excited residents of Philadelphia prepared to welcome home one of their hometown heroes. Mercy Street was decorated for the parade and Nick displayed Lanza's photos on his front window. He bought all the albums he could of Mario's first record. A warm-hearted Mario took time to visit his shop and shake Petrella's hand that day.

Nick was young and only in business for three years then, but he sold 4,000 of Mario's albums. He never saw so much money. He told me he and his mother bounced all that money on the kitchen table with joy.

Then came October 7th, 1959, Mario Lanza died at the age of 38. It stunned the world. Nick Petrella promises his grieving mother, Maria, he'd do everything possible to keep her son's name alive.

In 1962, Attorney John Papola, a classmate of Mario, incorporated The Mario Lanza Institute to raise funds to help young singers to further their musical education. Petrella, one of the five originators, became President two years later. Over 170 Scholarships grants have been awarded thus far with funds raised from the annual Mario Lanza Ball. Award winners now perform in many opera companies. The most successful is tenor Lando Bartolini, who sings at the Met and leading opera houses in the world.

From that small back-room in Petrella's Record Shop, the Mario Lanza Museum is now beautifully housed in the Settlement Music School, at 416 Queen Street, attracting visitors worldwide.

Under Nick Petrella's presidency along with the Board and Members, Mario Lanza now enjoys renewed stardom and loving remembrance. His records, movie videos and memorabilia are purchased gleefully from fans who have not forgotten.

And Mario's friend, Nick Petrella, likewise will never be forgotten. This caring, gentle, religious man, who's parting words were always: "GOD BLESS YOU," has enriched our lives. His large and pleasant presence will be missed. Always a gentleman, and truly a gentle man, Nick now walks with God. What can we say after we've said, "WE LOVE YOU, NICK?"

Top Left Photo: Al Martino Escorts Maria Lanza Cocozza (Mario Lanza's Mother) to the October 2, 1966 Annual Mario Lanza Ball.

Al Martino looks over the program With the late Maria Cocozza, Mario Lanza's mother with the late President Nick Petrella.

Bottom Photo: Joe Curreri, former P.R. Director for the Lanza Institute, Al Martino, the late Nick Petrella, President Of The Mario Lanza Institute.

The Mario Lanza Award was presented To Al Martino in 1973.

I RECALL

My Faith

Father Augustine Puchner, O.Praem
Words About My Friend Frankie Dee.

In my 18 years as a Catholic priest, I have been blessed with meeting many good people with whom I am able to share my life and ministry. Some of these people have become close and dear friends whose personal example of dedication to God and serving others gives me great inspiration in my own work. Frank DeSimone, "Frankie D." as he is called by his friends, is among that group of special people whom God has placed in my life as a witness to all that is good about living one's life with a purpose and passion that comes from faith in God and the desire to help others become the

person God wants them to be. Frankie's own life story is a wonderful example of what can happen when one truly hands one's life over to the power and care of God. This is the "God Concept" that Frankie lives by and shares with others as the key to success in life, especially dealing with the challenge to overcome addictions. Himself a recovering alcoholic, sober since 1985, Frankie now shares his experience and wisdom in several Alcoholics Anonymous groups and meetings. He has hosted meetings at St. John the Baptist Catholic Church in Costa Mesa, CA where I serve as pastor for over a decade, and that is how I have come to know Frankie as a special friend. Our collaboration in ministry has even made some local headlines here in Southern California, when, in the summer of 2014, I went to Frankie's Costa Mesa home to bless a special shrine he had constructed in a corner of his enclosed front yard. A reporter and cameraman were on hand to document the event, and Frankie's story and the story of the shrine – a monument to his sobriety in thanksgiving to God and the Blessed Virgin Mary – were the subject of a front page story of the local Daily Pilot. The article and pictures also ran in the LA Times.

Frankie and I have a regular monthly lunch appointment at one of our favorite little, family-run Italian restaurants not far from the parish. During our time of conversation we talk about the importance of God in our lives, how things are going in our ministries, and we share stories about our common interests and our "Wisconsin connection." I was born and raised in Milwaukee, and Frankie has relatives and ties to Kenosha, a small city south of Milwaukee near the Illinois border. Frankie tells wonderful stories about the "good old days" when faith and family were the foundation of everyone's life. I share my own happy memories of the past, and they we eventually get back to discussing the many challenges in our current times. And in all that we talk about, God is always mentioned. This is what makes my friendship with Frankie such a joy and inspiration – in the end, it all comes down to the God Concept. With Him, all things are possible! Frankie D. knows. And Frankie D. will tell you!

Crusade Christian Radio Features
The Frank E. Dee Show

Be sure to tune into the Frank E. Dee shows on Crusade Radio, it's a labor of love where you'll hear the all time great vocalists and big band sounds, and interesting talk about these great stars. For the past 14 or 15 years Crusade Radio has been featuring Frankie D. shows and Frankie is deeply honored to Mel Pyatt who is the owner of Crusade Radio as well as being his good friend. Crusade Radio is a Christian radio station carrying the message of our Lord God from all Christian churches. Mel Pyatt is the founder of Crusade Radio who believes that Christians need to listen to Christian radio. Crusade Radio is based in Visalia, California and heard the world over! You can view Crusade Radio web site through this URL www.crusaderadio.com

Some of the shows are 'Our People,' 'Great Tenors' and 'My own 'Frank E. Dee show' featuring music of the 40's up to the 60's. I am deeply proud to bring my own format to the radio audience of the good sounds, as my good friend, the late Bill Marlowe would say, of 'M-U-S-I-C, and not N-O-I-S-E'! The noise I refer to is Rap, heavy metal, and songs that had lyrics of hate, murder, and rape. Yet no one has ever come forth to stopp this crude and ghastly type of noise that has figured negatively into a society of crime, once it was allowed over the airwaves. My musical format is simple. Just beautiful songs of the 1940's to 60's, sung by the best vocal singers who have been cast aside by radio station management and program directors to make room for the likes of that noise. What a shame that such singers, as Perry Como, Al Martino, Don Cornell, Buddy Clark, Jerry Vale, Frank Sinatra, and Mario Lanza, do not receive equal time on radio stations across America as it used to be. It's time to bring back the good music and singers who sang songs with wonderful, meaningful lyrics that brought family values back into the field of enriched music and entertainment." You can thank the Gershwins, Cole Porter, Irving Berlin, and Harold Arlen who wrote great, everlasting music.

Frank E. Dee, was formerly a Boston radio host in the early 70's at the now defunct WHET radio station in Waltham, Massachusetts, where he hosted *The Frank E. Dee Show* and devoted his format to the great music of the 40's, through the 70's. He often said "I'd rather quit than play any of that garbage, known as noise, on my show." Dee was also a featured columnist with the Beacon Publishing Co. in Acton, Massachusetts, where he began his career as a feature writer from 1964 until 1977, when he moved to California. In the 90's he published the "American Liberty News", a conservative, editorial style newsletter for eight years. Today, he is the host of one of the 100 award winner web sites, "Golden Music Memories Of Yesteryear," at http://www.gmmy.com. He said, GMMY, (short for Golden Music Memories Of Yesteryear) receives over 47,500 visitors a month, the hits are way up there to be viewed. His main feature is promoting the great singers of the 40's, 50's, and 60's and the big bands. Frank E. Dee asks you to join him for a touch of nostalgia on Crusade Radio and Gmmy Radio."

I Met Frank At St. Mary's Church
By Judy Nibler Avritt

      The first time I met Frank De Simone in 1999 when I was leaving St Mary's By the Sea church after the 5 p.m. Mass and he was handling out church bulletins and was also singing a song at the same time. I don't recall the song but I remember it was an oldie, of course!!! I thought what a nice man to sing to the church patrons as they leave church.

      We see each other at the 5 p.m. mass. He is an usher and I am a Eucharistic Minister and we sit in the back of the church during Mass ready to do our duties. Over the course of the next five years we have grown to know each other very well and appreciate each other's sense of humor, he has a large list of stories being in the radio entertainment business and he knows a lot of show business people that go back to the

Judy Nibler Avritt

golden era when people were polite and you could understand what songs were about. Needless to say Frank doesn't care for "RAP." A group of us try to go to lunch now and then when we have time. Frank knows all of the "Hot Spots" in our area for good food and good prices. Sometimes he takes his friend who is a priest to lunch and I think Frank pays for the meal so he can go to confession at the same time and get a lengthy penance! Ha, ha.

Frank is a good guy and does a lot of service for the common good. He is always there to lend a helping hand to anyone who needs it providing they will also help themselves; he is not a pushover and expects people to be kind to one another. Frank has a great sense of humor and it is always in good taste. I treasure my friendship with Frank. God seems to bring good people into my life and that is a blessing, thank you Frank for being a part of my life.

Judy Nibler Avritt, Eucharistic Minister.

St. Mary's Church

My Miracles From God

Back in the early 80's when I was finally living a good sober life style due to turning my life and will over to the care of God and to a group of wonderful guys who helped me to stay sober, were there to help everyone to maintain a good clean spiritual sober life. These wonderful men became my close friends because they were there to help all of us who wanted to stay sober. It was my fourth year living a good sober life. The God concept was the most important part of living a spiritual life without the booze, and thanks be to God who turned my life around more so. I never had a problem in not believing in God, but it was through believing more so in God through this spiritual program for alcoholics has turned me into becoming a better and more honest human being. However I was never a thief or a crook or a trouble maker, I was a human being who always tried to help people even when I was living in a glass of booze. The change came in my life with these great men who lived spiritual lives and went all out to share their experience, strength, and hope. The topic was called "change in all your affairs and there is a God and you're not him." In sobriety my life became a miracle because I no longer had a desire to pick up a drink, and to me with God in my life, it was a miracle. Thanks to those men who helped new comers like me turn my life and will over to God.

In the year of 1988, I was getting ready for a vacation trip from California to Mexico to meet my brother and his wife who were from Boston. While I was at the Los Angeles airport getting ready to aboard my flight to Mexico I had a mild heart attack and the severe pain up my left arm was unbearable, unbeknownst to me I had a blood clot in my arm. An airport Nurse was quick to ask me to attend a local hospital in Los Angeles. I refused, and the nurse told me I would not live to arrive to my home city in Costa Mesa, California.

Talk about the miracle of having God in my life, I could have died at the airport. And of course my trip to Mexico was off, and the trip back to Costa Mesa, California where I was living was approximately a good 40 mile trip from the L.A. airport to Hoag hospital in Newport Beach. I was administered into the hospital and talk about miracles happening in my life, the Cardiologist was a heart specialist in a Boston hospital from my home state, Dr. James Shelburne.

He really saved my life by dissolving a blood clot in my left arm. I had spent seven days under his care. I talked about the great wonders and miracles of living a clean sober life under the care of Our Lord God who saved my life through the effort of a wonderful doctor, who I never forgot. I remember the nurses in the Hog Hospital telling me I was very fortunate to have Dr. Shelburne as my cardiologist, because he is one of the best in his field.

I will always be grateful to the elder men from my various alcoholic meetings who showered me with prayers and visits. I never, and I mean never met so many caring friends from our special miracle program of meetings.

He Loved God and Called Him 'George'

There were many wonderful spiritual men and women in the alcohol recovery meetings. I was truly honored to have met these now good friends who helped me and taught me the spiritual way in living one day at a time with God daily. One of my special friends, Don D., who at the time was in his 60's, spoke highly of God and our spiritual program. He always said "miracles do happen in these rooms, and if you keep coming back, life doesn't just get better, but it gets 'Gooder,' and 'Gooder' at one day at a time."

Don D., was well loved by all of us who knew him, he would always share his views with the whole group by telling us he always called God, 'George,' and when Don would go for long walks along the piers of Newport Beach, California, he would always tell the groups he enjoyed his long conversation with 'George.' He said having these talks with George always helped him solve any problem he may be going through. We were all amazed to hear Don talk about 'George' and for those of us new comers who didn't know who in the blazes he was talking about, I finally raised my hand to ask who 'George' was. Everyone who had been attending meetings for some years, already knew whom 'George' was to Don, but us new comers didn't know? When Don told us new comers who 'George' was, every new comer in the room burst out laughing. I never forgot what Don said; "George is my higher power and my God. Let me explain further, God who was my first Higher Power was 'Howard,' as in, Our Father, who art in Heaven, Howard be thy name." We all got the message. He was truly an impeccable caring man who would explain the smallest of sayings, especially when he was chairing the meeting, and he was quick to always ask; "Anybody from out of town? Out of state? Out of their minds? If so you're in the right place."

I was really blessed to have met such a spiritual man as Don D., who went out of his way to carry his spiritual message to all of us. Back in the 80's I got closer to those elder men who had good quality spiritual sobriety, I really wanted what they had. Men like Don D. and others like him, took me under their wings, they knew I wanted to stay sober and have God in my life daily, and whatever they told me to do I did without question. In my first two years I learned to say; "I became a part of rather than apart from." I wanted to start a new recovery meeting to help others get sober. I wanted to do something real different, with a new and different type of meeting called; 'A Podium Topic Participation.' I remember Don D., asking me, "what's holding you back?" Don said he would certainly carry the message to a lot of his friends. However I got bombarded by some who said; "we don't need any more Alcoholic Recovery meetings, we have enough of them." My answer to these gentlemen was, "you don't have to attend this new meeting." It was amazing that those who were against the new meeting were the first to show up. The new meeting started on a Wednesday night and in those years the meetings were an hour and a half long.

It was amazing or was it a miracle that a Pastor of a Lutheran church in California, who I met had asked me to start an Alcoholic Recovery meeting. I told the kind Pastor I did not belong to the Lutheran church. His quick remark was, 'well nobody's perfect.' He said there were people attending his church who had a drinking problem. He told me a Wednesday night meeting would be perfect and I could use one of the school classrooms. I was quick to present the entire introduction itinerary for the new podium topic meeting that allowed everyone who wanted to attend to share their topic from 3 to 4 minutes. On top of this great first meeting, I also added coffee and donuts and cold cuts for sandwiches. The turnout was about 25 people. And a lot of members were from various alcoholic recovery meetings. This meeting went on for years and then I finally left to start another new meeting at an alcoholic step house. I cannot thank the elderly men who, for over 20 years, stood behind me to start the new meetings.

Hello Mr Chairman, How are you this Friday morning ?

To Mr. Richard Grudens
I will try to write something concerning a close friend. Please remember me I am no writer.

I have had the pleasure of meeting Mr. Frank E. Dee about 15 years ago. At times, 10 years can seem like a different lifetime and a different world. I would like to think I get better with passing years. Well I hope so anyway. I can say this, it was a 'good thing' meeting Frank or as I refer to him jokingly as the 'Chairman.' It doesn't seem that time, health, or every day speed bumps have slowed him down at all.

He is active in not just one Church but two that I know about. For openers, St. Mary's By The Sea Catholic Church, on 10th street, in Huntington Beach Ca., where I have the pleasure in assisting in the masses together as ushers, also St John's Baptist Church in Costa Mesa, Ca. where he also gives his time by helping others in recovery. I didn't have the pleasure of knowing him in his early years which is my loss, but our paths have crossed. Who knows what God has planned for us? Maybe His plan was for Frank to share his experiences, and strength and hope with me, because you learn from the people you are with and I learned to simply enjoy the moment God has provided us.

I must hand it to Frank, I find it amazing how he is so active and finds time to run and operate Gmmy Radio, providing listening pleasure to everyone here in the U.S of A., all the way to the UK with the support of several radio hosts. Mr. Alan Brown, from the UK, is a man with a wealth of knowledge and is also very mechanical, who built his own airplane and is always doing something in his shop. From where I stand, I have a lot of respect for Frank, as a person always willing to share and give of himself by staying active and enjoying life. I hope other's may also have the experience that I had with Frank.

Thank you Mr. Richard Grudens for allowing me to share my feelings about a sincere good friend, Mr. Frank E. Dee It was a Pleasure.

Derrick Peront
Huntington Beach, California

My Dedication To Jesus
and The Blessed Mother
Yet Movies, Cassettes, Books,
About Alcoholics Accepted??

I have to vent. I never understood why some members of Alcoholic Anonymous resented my article about an altar that I dedicated to Our Lord Jesus Christ and the 'Blessed Mother,' which appeared in the Los Angeles Times, and the Costa Mesa Daily Pilot newspaper, the article was about a commitment I made to myself 31 years ago that if I ever got sober I would erect two statues - one of our Lord Jesus Christ, and the other statue of the Blessed Mother (who I affectionately call 'The Lady In Blue.') I guess the answer is that you will always find someone who is offended.

After the article appeared, I received a phone call from an anonymous alcoholic, who identified as a member of A.A. and said to me over the phone that I should not have not mentioned the Alcoholic Anonymous program in the newspaper. My question is why? After all there are many Hollywood films that mentioned the program such as "My Name is Bill W." made in 1989 Starring James Woods, Jo Beth Williams, James Garner and Gary Sinese." There are about 45 such films made about alcoholics - maybe more. It's an often mentioned recovery program that's synonymous when it comes to alcoholism. There are also a ton of books and cassettes about the issue and program that are sold by the thousands every year.

I am a recovered Alcoholic who worked as an instructor at a D.U.I. program for drunk drivers [Driving Under the Influence]. The students who were required to attend 'School Ten,' were sent by the Court system. Not only did the court system send these pupils, but they were also sent to A.A. Meetings to have their court card signed showing that they attended the A.A. Meetings. I sign these court cards weekly in two of my own meetings!!!!

To quote: "The way most people find themselves court-mandated to attend Alcoholics Anonymous meetings is by getting a drunk-driving conviction. In addition, A.A. is ordered for other alcohol-related convictions and in some domestic violence situations.

If you have been convicted of an alcohol-related offense, the court will sometimes offer you an alternative to going to jail. Because of jail overcrowding and the costs of keeping an offender incarcerated, many jurisdictions offer some kind of alternate or diversion program, such as A.A.. Many offenders end up in Alcoholics Anonymous simply because it's the only option that is free and is usually the most available of the options, with meetings in virtually every city and town. But for those who object to going to A.A., the other, more expensive options are available along with secular support groups in some areas." End of quote. Even the court systems recognize it as a program based on faith.

In reality I thank the United States Courts in sending drunk drivers to D.U.I. Classes, and to A.A. meetings to get their court cards signed by A.A. Secretaries because in my opinion anyone who is driving while intoxicated becomes a lethal weapon!

I have often laughed when I saw a photo of the first meeting of A.A. and the attendees were wearing masks and I didn't understand. Perhaps it was because of shame and anonymity. I though how in blazes can a masked person become a sponsor to an alcoholic who is looking for help?

In summary, there are many references to A.A. in the public, but there will always be people who object to the religious nature of the help that is received.

I Saw The Blessed Mother Cry

I shall never forget one of my trips back to my home town of Somerville, Mass. to visit my brothers and relatives and of course my radio friends. It was a hot day in the month of June in the year 2004. It was a day in my life I shall truly remember. My brother Leo knew I was active attending church in California since I had stuffed the plug into the booze jug. I remember Leo asking me several times if I still attend church weekly, and I told him I did. He asked me to take a ride with him through the neighborhood because he said he wanted to show me something special.

Well, I had know idea what he had in mind? I figured wherever he was going to take me I thought it might perhaps be to meet old friends. He drove about two miles from his home and approached an Old Catholic church called the 'Sacred Heart Church' that I remember as a boy which was located in Medford, Massachusetts next to the popular Tufts University College. I kept thinking to myself - why is he taking me here? As he pulled into the front driveway of this church, Leo asked me to look in front of the Rectory where a large statue of the Blessed Mother, whom I always called 'The Lady In Blue.' From a distance where he parked his car, he told me to look at the statue, and I did so, but I could see flowers and books and greeting cards, not knowing why?

As I began to walk with my brother closer to the statue I noticed many people taking photos of the Blessed Mother Statue. I asked my brother "why are there so many people with cameras taking photos of the Blessed Mother statue?" Leo said "wait until we approach the statue and look up at the face of the blessed Mother." When we approached the statue, Leo said "now look up at the face of the Blessed Mother." When I looked up, I saw tears rolling down from the statue's eyes and I felt a tremendous sorrowful feeling of sadness that I never ever encountered in my whole life. I started to cry and I felt the most sorrowful feelings of hurt. But I wasn't the only one who felt hurt and shed tears. I didn't want to leave the statue. I stood against a wall facing the 'Lady in Blue.' I just had such a sad feeling that I needed to remain. My brother had told me that news media men from the Boston daily papers and television news people had covered the event. Leo finally suggested we go for a cup of coffee at a nearby diner. I told him I needed to come back to the statue during the week as I made it a priority of my vacation to visiting the statue several times during the week.

When I told my relatives and friends that I had visited the Blessed Mother Statue, they too decided to come along with me as crowds were showing up daily, and photographers had been taking photos, and a lot of people also had been shedding tears of sadness. My dear friend who I grew up with as a teen, Mrs. Lorraine Parretti came with me to view the beautiful statue. I took numerous photos of the Blessed Mother Statue weeping, and back in 2005 I decided to write an article to send out to readers via the computer. More crowds started to show up. It was a sad time for a lot of the parishioners who attended the Sacred Heart church for years because the church was going to close and did so in July 2004.

For about a week I continued to visit the church and view the statue while it was still being displayed, and I felt it was going to be a matter of time that the statue of the Blessed Mother was going to be removed and sent to another church. It was a sad week meeting some nice people who too shed tears of sadness. I was told from some of the parishioners who believed the Blessed Mother statue shed tears of sorrow related to the Sacred Heart church closing down, and up to the time of closing a lot of people continued to show up every day.

Mrs. Parretti said "I never forgot what you and I saw." But, for some reason I was supposed to have seen the statue. I named the Blessed Mother "The Lady in Blue" because through her my life had turned 180 degrees with a terrific life of sobriety. I am grateful for the photos I had took to display with this article, and some of these photos are still being displayed on the website.

As we say in our recovery program to the unbelievers, I always point out 'there is a God, and you're not Him and He does work if and when you get out of his way. Amen!

Against Abortion!
Gmmy Radio and Websites
Have Always Been Against Abortions
"Life Begins At Conception and Ends At Natural Death!!"

While ABORTIONS continue to be the so called 'IN THING' in our society. God must be angry with the American people, and rightfully so, and without doubt, He must be angry at our President, along with the government leaders, who supported the passage of "PARTIAL-BIRTH ABORTION!"

God's commandments have been forgotten while the American people lean on their own understanding. It all began on June 17, 1963, 52 years ago, when powerful old men in judicial robes took God out of the classroom and America has not been the same since. Since prayer has been removed, condoms and sex have become top subjects in our school system. And recently murders have been committed on school grounds. A Good Reminder: "For My people are destroyed for lack of knowledge; because thou has rejected knowledge, I will also reject thee, that thou shalt be no priest to me: seeing that thou has forgotten the law of God, I will forget thy children."

A brief review of the past 40 years graphically illustrates how America has departed from the narrow path that goes through the narrow gate and has instead, been absorbed in extravagance and waywardness to a degree that could have scarcely been imagined in 1963. Our nation is wracked by drug use, aids, alcoholism, homelessness, pornography, child abuse, violent crimes, abortion, teen pregnancy, rape and now date rape, and promiscuity. I would also add that rap music creates a destructive state of mind. Our President has been noted to lie from both sides of his mouth, and seems to have his own personal version of the bible, "The Gospel According To The President," who tries to play the role of God with life. Why is it that politicians do not understand the view of "Life Begins at Conception and Ends at Natural Death?"

In the meantime, the American people are on a pleasure binge. Hedonism is rampant! "Live for today, for who knows what tomorrow brings!" "Do your own thing" – "Protect your own butt--?"

"If it feels right, do it"--. "Truth is what you make it" -- "Do unto others, then split" -- "If it's free, it's for me" -- "Don't do as I do, but do as I say." The well-being of the family has deteriorated as divorce has skyrocketed. Up over 200 percent since the 1960's, and out-of-wed-lock births are up over 400 percent.

The American people are paying dearly. Humanism is in the saddle. For all too many, God has become for them the material things with which they have surrounded themselves, or which they seek to acquire. Where the people renounce the true God, a false god will be provided. Indeed, the State instead of the Lord will be our shepherd.

Today, there is a vicious no holds-barred assault against us as Alexander Solzhenitsyn wrote, "To destroy a country you must first cut its roots. If America's roots are in Judeo-Christian values and traditions, they have in large measure been severed." When one considers America today, they cannot help recognize the appalling parallel. America is on the same precipitous slope! And our government is not making the situation any better!

Americans can pray that these roots can be restored and cling to God's promise: "If my people, which are called by my name, shall humble themselves and pray and seek my face, and turn from their wicked ways; then will I hear from heaven, and will forgive their sin and will heal their land." 2 Chronicles 7:14

To christian pastor John Hagee, from the Corner Stone Ministries, in Texas: "We will save an owl in a tree! Yet destroy a baby in the womb of a mother!" "Yesterdays hopes and dreams are filled with hate and no love!" Pastor Hagee who pulls no punches when it comes to ABORTIONS, also delivers a powerful message to politicians in Congress, and the Senate members who supported "PARTIAL-BIRTH ABORTIONS."

Take Back Our Country!

Restore America to good moral leadership in our government! Stop supporting pro-choice leadership! Support pro-lifers 100 percent!

A message worth repeating.

Gmmy Radio & Gmmy Websites Endorses
Pro-Life Worldwide
And
California's Dr. Fritz Baumgartner, MD

In October of 2011 Southern California Catholic churches kicked off their annual 'Pennies From Heaven' collection, a wonderful supportive program for 'Pro-Life.' The churches ask parishioners to bring in all their loose change [and bills] for the month of October to support several Orange County Pro-Life organizations. I am deeply honored to take part of this program in helping with collections at St. Mary's By The Sea Catholic Church under the guideship of two wonderful Catholic priests; Rev. Joseph Lauan Nguyen and Rev. Eamon Mackin.

"When Does Life Begin"?

For those who question "when does life begin"? I know that Dr. Fritz Baumgartner has the answer to your question. I have always believed God Gives Life and God Takes Life.... Therefore In God We Trust, And Politicians We Don't! Thank you Dr. Fritz Baumgartner.

The Hippocratic Oath was anti-abortion:

"When I graduated from the UCLA School of Medicine in 1984, we took the Hippocratic Oath, which states, "I will not give to a woman an instrument to produce abortion. With purity and holiness I will pass my life and practice my art." The Hippocratic Oath, explicitly and implicitly, eliminates abortion as an option."

Pro-Life America
Saving babies and families from abortion!
Life Begins at the Beginning

(A Doctor Gives the Scientific Facts on When Life Begins)

We can approach abortion from many perspectives: Biological, embryological, genetic, philosophical, social and economic, at the very least. As for the first three – my approach as a scientist, physician, surgeon, and simply someone who finished medical school, is factual.

There is no more pivotal moment in the subsequent growth and development of a human being than when 23 chromosomes of the father join with 23 chromosomes of the mother to form a unique, 46-chromosomed individual, with a gender, who had previously simply not existed. Period. No debate.

Be Sure To Read Dr. Baumgartner's complete article by visiting the following web site:

http://www.prolife.com/life_begins.html

To Dr. Fritz Baumgartner: Bravo to you, and God bless you. Thank you for having guts, courage, and common sense. Politicians and lawyers will be politicians and lawyers. But how in heaven's name can a doctor participate in such atrocities? It is akin to Dr Josef Mengele of Auschwitz concentration camp who did horrifying experiments on twins and then dissected their bodies for research. (He escaped the Nazi war crimes, and guess what he did next? He became an expert abortionist in Argentina). Planned Parenthood and the Nazi ideology truly, truly originate from the same evil fruit.

We need more doctors like Dr. Frank Baumgartner to take a stand against abortions and stop the sale of baby organs! GMMY radio and websites have always been against abortions and now the sale of baby organs!! Why don't the court system and politicians stop the sale of baby organs!!!! Shame on you disgusting politicians and judges allowing such terrible disasters!!!!

SoberLife USA: TinaRuck, FritzBaumgartner, Me and ChrisTiemann.

Dr. Baumgartner performed a triple by pass on me several years ago. He's a very spiritual doctor and a good friend. He and his crew from SoberLife USA took me to lunch - pictured above.

GMMY Radio and Golden Music Memories of Yesteryear Websites Have Always Supported Pro Life

"Before I formed you in the womb, I knew you, and before you were born, I consecrated you." Jeremiah 1:5

I am grateful and thankful to the late great radio host Bill Marlowe who was very supportive in helping me get the word "Pro-Life" out over the years. He was one of those people with a big back bone who took a stand on his radio show as well as our American Liberty Newsletter.

Bill an yours truly, were supporters of the Pro Life movement. The Pro Choice movement would agree that infanticide is definitely wrong. There is no question that it is murder. Nevertheless, what is the difference between procedures which murs a baby one month before birth, from a procedure which seeks to murder a baby one month after birth? A woman's womb should not become a place of death, but of life. Just as the right to murder a human being outside of the womb should never be legalized, neither should the right to end life in the womb.

Women are often heard, who endorse and support abortion, that they are for "Pro Choice" or "it should be a woman's choice." In reality they do have a choice! The choice is not to abort the baby being carried in their womb! If they are raped and end up pregnant, they should have the baby, put it up for adoption, rather than have the baby killed! There is no support in any bible that God, our creator, condones abortion. These pro choice laws are man made, and certainly not laws made by God. While many will claim that God does not exist, such individuals certainly would never advocate the ending of a life. Nor would anyone ever think to be an advocate for the right for one to have the choice to end the life of a human being. We too were unborn children who lived in the wombs of our mothers. We had the opportunity to continue with our natural lives, so why shouldn't others? The unborn child is indeed a human being. His and her life must be protected.

To save the life of an unborn child may require sacrifice, and it may not be easy or convenient, but life should no be a matter of choice.

"Truly you have formed my inmost being; you knit me in my mother's womb. I give you thanks that I am fearfully, wonderfully made; wonderful are your works." Psalm 139: 13,14

GMMY Radio and websites have always supported pro-life 100 percent. We also endorse and support all websites on the worldwide web who are pro-life.

I RECALL

Sobriety

"Frankie, There Is A God, And You're Not Him And He Will Help You If You Get Out Of His Way!"

In most Italian homes, homemade 'VINO' known in English as wine, was made every October, and as far as I can remember my father always made 3 or 4 barrels of wine and as I grew older I learned to crush the grapes by cranking a hand machine one bushel at a time. The worse part of the job was lugging these 36 pound wooden crates from the side walk all the way into the back yard and down our bulkhead cellar stairs into the basement. In those days a crate of 'Zinfandel' grapes sold for $1.50. I remember there were always 40 crates or more to be crushed for fermenting. After the fermenting process, the wine was drained out of the fermenting barrels and put into other barrels for drinking and stored in a wine room behind a locked door. The remains of the fermented grapes were put into a grape press and pressed then added to the barrels for clearage. The process of making homemade wine was indeed a tough job, but the pleasure of drinking wine was wonderful for a drinker like me.

I always thought everyone drank Italian homemade wine because everyone who visited my parent's home had a glass in their hand. I have to admit, my father never made a bad barrel of wine, his secret was buying sweet grapes that were shipped from California. He would go from car train to car train to taste each batch to make certain the grapes he was going to buy were real sweet, which produced a good flavor and a high alcohol content. He also made Italian Muscatel - it was called Muscato in Italian [White wine], and what a kick that 'Muscato' had.

Every Italian family we knew and also friends of my father, made homemade wine - there was always a competition among them - all bragging that they made the best. In my case I drank any kind of wine as long as it was homemade and sweet. As far as I can remember I always drank the wine as a teenager. However my father and brothers rarely drank but a few glasses of wine with meals, they never allowed wine to be a priority in their lives.

Booze For An Alcoholic
Is An Insidious Disease

I drank wine daily as a young boy, and later in my teens I graduated to drinking beer and whiskey. I became a full blown alcoholic, not knowing this disease was labeled as an insidious disease of destruction. I have to admit, I never got into trouble, but drinking was my trouble. I never lost a job, due to my drinking. However drinking does cause divorces and I went through two divorces due to my constant drinking and boozing around the bars and attending parties. It's a ridiculously terrible life style for anyone who drank like I did. Thankfully I was not one to drive a car fast, and for some strange reason, or miracle, I didn't get into an accident or run a red light and kill a pedestrian.

I always had deep sense that someone or something was watching over me, because there were too many good turns in my drinking life that I could not explain. With my constant daily drinking I should have been dead. Any practicing alcoholic drinker would understand the crying, the shakes and even spitting up blood. I remember having the shakes so bad, that I could not hold a cup of coffee in my hands. And if you don't believe this, ask any sober alcoholic who drank daily day and night?

The truth is any alcoholic drinker who drank daily will make promises to quit the booze, but when it comes to putting the plug in the jug, it never happened for this recovered alcoholic while I still was drinking daily. And how many times did I make promises of putting the plug in the jug? Dozens and dozens of times! Booze became my higher power, it was a road filled of self will run riot.

'Change' In All Our Ways

From the very first meeting I attended along with other new comers we were told we had to 'change' all of our ways, by getting rid of those old character defects and short comings. The old timers would say: "When we tell you about 'change', we don't mean what you have in your pockets. The change we mean is you have to change your life style by getting rid of those old defects by turning your will over to the care of God. They were right - we became more spiritual as time went on. By 'changing' our views, life became 100 percent better than when we were living in a bottle of booze, and we were reminded 'In God we trust, all others are questionable.'

I learned the importance of turning 'our will over to the care of God,' and trying very hard, with the rest of the group, to change our own character defects to become a better person than what we were like when living in a bottle. Thankfully, during my drinking days, I was not a thief, crook or one who took people for granted. All of the new comers were told to write about our personal defects and short comings, an inventory, if you will, and prayer was to be included this list, which we then had to share with our own personal sponsor. One sponsor used to say: "remember there is a God, and you're not Him, and He does work if you get out of His way." We were often reminded of those words. But the sponsors were 100 percent right! Through prayer and God's grace, we were able to change and become sober and live a healthy life.

I was fortunate to obtain a sponsor who walked the talk of spirituality. Through prayer, I have changed my life one day at a time. I have never had the desire to pick up a drink. I never rejected social drinkers, as I always believed there is nothing wrong with anyone who enjoys a glass of wine, or a high ball as long as it doesn't turn into a gallon a day addiction. Many a marriage has gone down the tubes because of alcoholism. I see and I hear these problems every day, I even receive phone calls asking for help. My answer to those who have called me is purely simple - 'you have to change!'

At my recovery meetings numerous members made it known that foul language was not permitted. However, there were always a few attendees with foul mouths who would swear, curse, and assert - "we'll swear anytime we wish, and there's no one going to stop us." Whoa! That was the wrong this to say in front of the leaders who had years of good clean spiritual sobriety. They escorted the foul mouth cursers out the door without any problem whatsoever. The two gentlemen who removed the cursing duo said; "when you grow up and clean up your act without any foul language, we may allow you to come into our meeting, but until that time, you are not allowed in this group meeting."

The old timers, as we called them, were a beautifuly spiritual group who would go all out to help anyone of us who needed their support. But when it came to foul mouth new comers, they were always shown the door. Their motto was; "we don't need to hear garbage language from newcomers or whoever, because this program is a program of 'Change."

A Message Sobriety Is A Wonderful Life

I was taught from my elder spiritual members "there is no such word in Webster's dictionary called 'Alcoholicwasim.'

But you will find the word Alcoholism. And if I had continued on my boozing journey, you can rest assured this biography would not have been published because I would have passed away. The truth is that I turned my life and my will over to the care of God, and thanks be to God the Father and His blessed Son Jesus Christ, I was able to turn my life away from booze and the life style of living in a glass of alcohol every day.

There are so many wonderful miracles that come to those who have a problem with alcohol and who decide to put the plug in the jug or as we say quit drinking. I guarantee those of you who decide to put the plug into the jug, your life will become a fantastic, enjoyable spiritual life, and you will meet new friends who will be a big part of your life. I have to honestly admit I came to believe in God without any problem, and by turning my life over to the care of God it became a daily miracle. I found that prayer is the world's greatest wireless connection, and through God, numerous wonders have happened and the miracles continue on and on. One of the greatest sayings among recovered alcoholics is, and I quote: "what we forget, God remembers and what we disregard God disposes." In all honesty, without living in a glass of booze, your life will become as we say "easy does it and the going becomes great."

Even in sobriety, I met people whom I first trusted and found out later were liars, takers, and greedy for gain. As strange as it seemed God did remove those people from my life, because I was also forewarned by my sponsors and close spiritual friends to be aware of these types and to walk away from because I knew they were not honest. So I remained closer to my real friends who lived a spiritual life, and taught me the roads of spirituality. I have learned through my elder peers in my 31 years of sobriety; "it's okay to make an honest mistake, because mistakes are our teachers, they help us to learn."

As I look back in time, I'm grateful for the wonderful sober life I shared with good sponsors who then became my close friends, you might say they were like parents and close brothers to me. There was so much clean humor, and laughs and one particular saying that always gave me a chuckle - "are you busted, disgusted, and can't be trusted?"

Believe it or not I continue to pass that wonderful saying to new comers, which does brings a laugh to the men and ladies coming to meetings. I learned to live 'one day at a time' and to become a better sober human being. One of my favorite sayings was "the absence of profanity will offend no one, profanity is not a sign of spiritual growth."

Me in the camera booth rewinding the 35 meter films This was the best place to drink beer while learning a trade [how wrong was I]. At 17 years of age I was working part time in the evenings as a Film Projectionist at the Teele Square Theater in Somerville, MA.

Jim Campbell
One Of Maine's Pop Country Western Singers

Jim Campbell, a close friend and I, were raised on the same street and we both attended the same schools starting out in kindergarten up until we both quit school at age 16. When Jim was 8 years old his grandfather made sure Jim took guitar lessons, which meant he could not go out to play with the local boys until he did his hourly daily lesson. We both lived and enjoyed the great neighborhood where all families helped one another, especially in the war years, and growing up as young boys we still talk about the fun teen years when we used to steal apples and pears from neighbors who grew gardens and fruit trees. The neighbors always insisted that we didn't steal their fruits and veggies from their garden, they said we should just ask them to share some of their fruits, because that way we would not destroy their trees by pulling down branches and breaking them to reach the fruit. We still talk about those days when everyone cared for one another and when fruits and vegetables were five cents each.

So, had it not been for Jim Campbell I would not have lived - due to my alcoholism? It was Jim who came all the way from Sydney, Maine to take me to my very first meeting at a local halfway house. It was a Friday night meeting and I was still half way drunk and shaking like a leaf and I was filled with tears and shame, but when Jim took me into that room filled with men and women who were recovered alcoholics, they welcomed me in with open arms, and when it was time for the meeting to start at 8 p.m the leader of the meeting asked all the new comers to stand and identify themselves, and when it came to me I stood up saying "my name is Frankie Dee and I'm drunk." The whole room broke out laughing - I didn't have to admit I was drunk, because I smelled like a brewery. It was in this halfway house where the owner and other members, took me under their wings of sobriety and became my close friends for 31 years. Thanks be to Jim Campbell who went all out to help me to live a beautiful sober life.

This Photo was taken in my first year and a half of sobriety , Jim Campbell came out to visit me to celebrate my recovery birthday. In 2014, Jim celebrated his 38th year of sobriety. My sobriety is a beautiful miracle thanks be to God, and to Jim Campbell

who took me to my very first alcoholic recovering meeting. I never forgot the popular saying I learned from those wonderful rooms and "I Found God" to which my recovered alcoholic friends would laugh and remind me that "Frankie, God was never lost, You were."

Jim Campbell's became popular with his five piece country western band which played, all over the state of Maine, singing popular country-western songs. It wasn't long before one of Maine's popular television stations, WLBCTV-2, offered Jim a fourteen month show where he would play and sing his country western songs throughout Maine. Jim was always booked throughout Main in the many night clubs.

Now, at age 80, Jim Campbell still sings and plays for seniors and remains popular through his gift, and, as he said, "had it not been for my sobriety, I too would have been deceased, because that's what the power of booze can do." I thank God for my sobriety and my home and my good friends." Jim also started meetings for friends that needed help as well as for a local jail. He always makes time to help others. Jim Campbell sobered up in 1978.

Today, we stay in close touch and Jim would often come to California and stay at my home. We talk about the good old days when we used to lie about our age to get into a bar to buy a glass of beer, and in those days a glass of beer cost ten cents for an eight ounce glass of any named brand tap beer. A shot of whiskey went for 30 to 40 cents for a big short. When Jim comes to visit here, we go to meetings together and talk about the price of what booze and beer cost back in the early 1940's. When we talk at meetings today about what booze and beer used to cost, the attendees look at us as though we were telling a lie, because now a shot of whiskey will cost from $8 to $10 dollars, and a bottle of beer is anywhere from five dollars and up. Yikes! We would not be able to afford those prices to get drunk, and we thank God, who helped Jim and I to become sober.

Amen!

Booze Did Not Open the Gates to Heaven to Let Me In

It is a known fact that booze did not open the gates of Heaven to let me or any other alcoholic in, instead booze opened the gates of hell to let us out, and that is a known fact for this former practicing alcoholic. Booze will always bring misery if one drinks long and hard enough daily. Thanks be to God who turned my life around. If you have read some of the articles in this book about my personal life of living in a bottle of booze daily, you'll know that I have seen a lot of my friends die from the weapon of alcohol as I called it, because booze will destroy one's life. Booze destroys marriages and brings loss of work for the practicing alcoholic. Over the past 30 years of living a sober spiritual life, I have attended over a half a dozen funerals (both men and women) whose deaths were caused by alcoholism.

Without any doubt, sobriety comes from the Grace of God, if anyone out there has a real drinking problem and is willing to turn their life and their will over to the care of God daily, they will get sober. And I am living proof and I'm going into my 31st year of enjoying a clean-cut humorous life with my fellow colleagues who also have reached out to help me turn my life around 180 degrees. The God concept is very important in our lives. I hear all sorts of off the wall stories from girls and guys who complain even in their 8th year of sobriety. The answer is simple; if they were to turn their lives and their will over to God and let Him and only Him run the show they would find great comfort for themselves. I was always taught by my elder peers and I quote what they taught me "prayer is an action and grace is what God gives us when we don't deserve, and mercy is when God doesn't give us what we do deserve." Whatever church I visited be it Baptist, Catholic or any denomination, I always kneeled to pray to our Lord God to thank Him for my sobriety, and I learned "in the name of Jesus every knee should bow or kneel, of those in heaven, and of those on earth, and of those under the earth."

Often I have been asked why I decided to get into a spiritual recovery program? My answer has never changed. I came into a spiritual program because I was 'sick and tired of being sick and tired' of the shakes, and throwing up blood. And I learned I did not like the guy I saw in the mirror who looked back at a blood shocking red eyed drunk - 'me'. I recall when I worked for Earle W. Tuttle, former owner of the Beacon Publications weekly newspapers in Acton, Massachusetts, how on earth this gentle spiritual giant put up with yours truly when I

W.C. Fields

arrived on the job smelling like a bar. He presented me with a big photo of W.C. Fields, because I used to mimic the way W.C. Fields talked and on the picture was Mr. Fields popular statement "thou shalt not kill anything less than a fifth" and "thou shalt not covet thy neighbor's house unless they have a well-stocked bar of booze." Today that same photo hangs in our GMMY Radio studio as a wise reminder. When I finally sobered up, Earle would often come with his wife to visit me in California.

A New Beginning

I was truly blessed by having two wonderful men who went all out to help me become sober. Harold Richards and Frankie Ivanovich. "I'll never forget the welcome I received from a house filled with recovered alcoholics and their board members when I attendeed a particular Friday night meeting. The date was April 12 1985. The room was packed with other new comers who desired a sober life style. When that first meeting started everyone in the room identified themselves by stating 'my name is so and so and I am an alcoholic."

After everyone had identified themselves the crowd of new members were heartily welcomed with enthusiastic applause. Frankie wasn't aware these meetings began with a prayer and closed with the Lord's Prayer.

"At that first meeting I attended the room looked so dark and I felt I could hide myself sitting against the wall full of newcomers on both sides of me. How foolish my thinking was that being a new comer I could hide from anyone. I was ashamed of what booze did to this alcoholic. I was so nervous and afraid to be called on to speak about my drinking problem, and when it came time for me to speak, I stood up and said; 'My name is Frankie D, and I'm drunk!' I was answered with unexpected applause and laughter and a big shout of 'welcome to sobriety.' I was never so scared in my entire life identifying myself publicly as a drunk. Guess what? The fear of attending this first Friday night meeting was somewhat lifted after I had stood and identified as being a full-blown drunk. A warm comfort came over me, and my fear subsided."

After the hour-and-a-half meeting ended, me and other eligible members, approached me and wished me an honest welcome to my first meeting. Harold, the owner of the halfway house greeted me with a big smile and clasped my hand. For me, this was the beginning of a long friendship. Harold's first words were "just remember there is a God, and he will work in your life if you get out of his way." This too was the very first time I was introduced to Frankie I., known as The Count of Newport Beach, one great humorous human being who took me under his wing. Harold, Frankie I, and a guy named Mike, became my alcoholic sponsors who also taught me God's concept of the spiritual steps to sobriety.

After each meeting different groups would go for coffee and pie or perhaps a sandwich at a local and friendly coffee and pastry shop. And the program of spirituality would become a topic among members who attended those meetings. Clean-cut humor became the favorite topic. Elder members of the groups never permitted the use of foul language in the restaurant. As a matter of fact such language was unheard of compared to what goes on during the present years. Today it's shoved down our throats through television and Hollywood films, and rarely do alcoholic members attend movie of this present generation due to the violence and the swearing.

If one or two members didn't show up at a special meeting, another member would call you at your home to see if you were okay. They showed their concern towards the newcomer, and if you needed a ride to get to a meeting they would be certain to come pick you up to take you to their own house where they frequently hosted weekly meetings. Their point was well established, as they always - "cared about one another."

L-R: Harold Richards, Me and Frank Ivanovich

"There's Magic in These Rooms"

In the beginning, I was attending a lot of recovery meetings. You get to the point where you being to relax and eventually look forward to attending, because of what you learn and by enjoying "the old-timers" who walked the talk, as they used to say, and what they share and their views on how they remained sober.

Every one of those elder spiritual men and women would always say "You can't get sober and stay sober without God in your life." This is a spiritual program designed for the alcoholic person who has a drinking problem." I certainly could relate to what was being said, but I kept my ears open and my mouth shut, as I was willing to do anything I was advised to do. Most new comers will do the same.

I went to these meetings because I wanted to become sober and change my life style from 'boozing and losing' while I turned my life over to God, and to learn and join with the winners who had long time spiritual sobriety, some for up to 40 years. Most of the meetings I attended were filled with people who worked their pro-gram daily, by praying to God. There was a gentleman called Len B. who always said at the beginning of every meeting I attended - "there's spiritual magic in all these rooms, and if you keep coming back you'll enjoy the miracles." So right was Len B. He always shared stories about the miracles God could perform for those of us who are willing to turn our daily lives over to God.

I never had a problem believing in God, my problem was during my drinking career, I was too busy to say "thank you God for another day above ground." I always believed God was watching over me, because the way I drank, I should have been dead. When I started to sober up and once again feel like a healthy person, I lost the desire to drink. Once, while I was drinking and crying in my bedroom, I recall that I did not want to go on with life, due to the booze that became my higher power. I have been blessed with wonderful friends who reached out to help me by attending meet-ings and praying.

There were a lot of new-comers that joined those Friday night recovery meetings, who had a hard time believing in almighty

God, and turning their lives and will over to His care. A lot of these new comers use to beat themselves up mentally and did not wanting to hear any topics about God. Those very same men could not enjoy a sober moment and they shared their views of unbelief in God, and so their lives became unmanageable. Eventually, in weeks to come many of them left the meetings and went back to drinking, but those who remained and continued attending meetings, were turned around through their belief in God, and with the help of a sponsor who walked them through their problems.

Len B., who would say "get out of the stinking thinking. Get into prayer and meditation, they are our principal means of conscious contact with God." I wanted what these people had. It was called change your ways and become the person God wants you to be because he loves you.

Always remember, if booze doesn't bring you to your knees, sobriety will.